SURVIVOR

AGNEEPATH (The path of fire)

Tu na thakega kabhi,

Tu na thamega kabhi,

Tu na mudega kabhi.

Kar shapath! Kar shapath! Kar shapath!

Agneepath! Agneepath! Agneepath!

Translated

You will not ever tire,

You will not ever stop,

You will not ever turn back.

Take this oath! Take this oath! Take this oath!

The path of fire! The path of fire! The path of fire!

Courtesy: Excerpt from poem 'AGNEEPATH' by Dr. Harivansh Rai Bachchan

SURVIVOR

AMITABH BACHCHAN

RAJNNI LALSINGAANI

SURVIVOR
AMITABH BACHCHAN

First published in Australia by RAJNNI LALSINGAANI 2018
www.survivor-thebook.com

Prepublication Data Service details available from
The National Library of Australia
ISBN: 978-0-6483662-0-1 (pbk)
ISBN: 978-0-6483662-1-8 (ebk)

Typesetting and design by Publicious Book Publishing
Published in collaboration with Publicious Book Publishing
www.publicious.com.au

Disclaimer: This book has been written to express the essence of an incident in time, the most compelling moments, the memories and emotions associated with that incident as it happened.

This is my recollection of living through a very significant event of Mr. Bachchan's life, helped by my collection of newspaper cuttings. All attempts have been made to acknowledge sources of articles, both in print and online, that I would have read or referred to over these years.

The entire episode of the Coolie accident from 1982 was reported in the media several times with many articles written over the years. However, most of what has been reproduced here are from my perspective and the way in which my mind processed this information. I have tried to recreate events, locales, and conversations from my memories of them. The information I have read and retained has been collected over decades and the 'reference page' at the end of this book lists website links and newspapers that I would have read or referred to for this book and for quotes by Amitabh Bachchan.

There are countless books and articles available that do justice to Amitabh Bachchan's work, his achievements, and his career. My attempt here is not to chronicle the life of the great actor and an exemplary human being, but to explore how his personality and struggle through the many challenges of life showcases the character of a survivor.

DEDICATION

To my Mum and Dad, it's impossible to thank you adequately for everything you've done and I don't think I ever acknowledged that while you were alive.

From loving me unconditionally to raising me in a stable household, you instilled traditional values of integrity and honesty, of respecting fellow humans and taught us, your children, to celebrate and embrace life. I could not have asked for better parents or role-models.

I would also like to dedicate all profits from this book to charity. In Bombay (Mumbai), people often don't have the means to pay for resources and accommodation while their loved ones are treated in public hospitals. The objective is to provide parents, relatives, and friends with the facilities, advice and contacts they need while taking care of loved ones in hospitals or specialized care centers. I will collaborate with and provide funds to the local charities and associations that work with these hospitals.

The ones who look after their family and friends are also survivors, as equally as the people who overcome their sickness and ailments.

FOREWORD

(Amitabh Bachchan)

May 21, 2018

Life is difficult for everyone; everyone has bad days. Everyone has trouble in their life. Sickness and trouble and worry and love, these things will trouble you at every level of life.

Life is so precious, it can be lost in an instant. 'Health' and 'Life' are not valued till sickness or life threatening accidents occur.

The greatest glory in living, lies not in never failing, but in rising every time we fail. Hope is important because it can make the present moment less difficult to bear. The difference between stumbling blocks and stepping stones, is how we use them. Next to trying and winning, the best thing is trying and failing. It's important to remember that setbacks, failures and tragedy are a part of life. Whether we manage to find joy and success in the daily struggle of life is largely dependent on our ability to persevere through even the toughest adversity without ever giving up.

Pain is to be embraced and burned as fuel for our journey to success. The book 'Survivor' serves as a reminder of **my** "deliverance" – of God's presence and the life I owe to him, my family, and all those who rallied around me.

Those who read between the lines will find messages that go deeper. My prayers and blessings for the grand success of this publication. May it be a source of encouragement and hope to all those who read it.

With best wishes

Amitabh Bachchan

PROLOGUE

Circa 1982 – At the set of the movie 'Coolie' in Bangalore, India

On 24 July 1982, while filming Coolie, in the University Campus in Bangalore, Mr. Amitabh Bachchan suffered a near fatal intestinal injury during the filming of a fight scene with co-actor Puneet Issar. Mr. Bachchan was performing his own stunts in the film. One scene required him to fall on a table and then onto the ground. However, as he jumped towards the table, the corner of the table struck his abdomen, resulting in a splenic rupture and a significant loss of blood. Rushed to the hospital, he required an emergency splenectomy and remained critically ill in hospital for many weeks. At times, he was close to death. The response from the public was overwhelming; fans prayed in temples and offered to sacrifice limbs to save him. Later, long queues of well-wishing fans waited outside the hospital where he was recuperating.

Circa 2018 – At a café by 'Glenelg beach' in Adelaide, Australia

After a spree of spring cleaning, I was going through a folder of my old journals, notes, and birthday cards. I was listening to the waves and sipping coffee when I came across an old frayed notebook. My heart skipped a beat; I immediately knew what it was. My one and only scrapbook. As I started flipping through the pages, the memory of those days flashed through my eyes and I was transported to the past, once again experiencing that incident as it happened.

But for my Mum's advice to record my experience of the event in a memory book, this information would never have lasted the last three decades. Between varied jaunts to different countries and multiple moves across the world, this little notebook has survived. I can now bring you Mr. Amitabh Bachchan's incident as it happened, through clippings and reports from the newspapers in 1982. I hope to share with all of you the trials and tribulations of a young, naïve, and smitten girl living the trauma of her idol.

CONTENTS

INTRODUCTION

Why do I want to write about Amitabh Bachchan?

What sets him apart from other larger than life movie stars?

What is about him that inspires, evokes, and generates awesome idolization?

Obviously, there is much more to him than his talent, performances, and histrionics.

What I am referring to here are facets of a man in real life outside of reel life. His personality, his characteristics, his humanitarian traits, how he conducts himself in everyday life situations, in a world of you and me.

Mind you, I am not talking about Amitabh Bachchan as if I have known him personally. On the contrary, I have had only one occasion to meet with him and that too, very briefly. But one does not have to meet Amitabh in person to be so affected by his persona and enigmatic personality. His life story as known to the world has been filled with instances of struggle, persistence, and courage. This has resonated with me since I was young, staying with me and providing inspiration as I faced my own difficult moments in life. For that, I thank him. I hope that this book, and Amitabh's journey, inspire you as it has for me.

In this book, you will see and read for yourself what it is that makes this man a legend. It's not what a person says, but rather what he does and how he does it, that speaks volumes about the man, his inherent integrity, his drive, his motivation and his ethical standards. He has the DNA of a fighter that sets him distinctly apart. An indomitable spirit combined with kind thoughts and deeds.

After all, actions speak louder than words and his actions have spoken. The world has seen Amitabh Bachchan and the verdict is unanimous: His is the spirit of an "indestructible survivor".

I now have a daunting task ahead of me; start putting the words together to bring to life the story of a man, a persona, a charisma, a phenomenon, a revolution, a sensation, a superstar, a happening, a cult, a brand, and an idol.

I've been thinking about how the story needs to be told, tossing and turning through sleepless nights. Every stroke of my keyboard seemed unequipped to tell the story the way it deserved to be told.

But then I thought, it shouldn't be so. I have been following this man since I was a teenager. I don't exactly remember when the addiction started, but the admiration grew from a small spark and before I knew it, I was hooked. To whet my emotional appetite, I was lapping up gossip (very little), titbits (only rarely) and his movies (thankfully, many available) over and over again.

In those days (the 70s and early 80s), current movies were not shown on TV, nor were there enough video cassettes to go around. To get my weekly fix of watching 'him', I had to do the rounds of cinemas, watching repeats over and over again. Luckily for me, my entire family were fans of his movies and almost to the same extent as myself. It meant I could drag my Mum along to watch (since I was not 'allowed' to go to movies with friends).

On Sundays, we would rent a VCR player for the day and choose three to four films to watch. They would almost always be Amitabh Bachchan films. His films helped bridge our generation gap: no matter what else within my family we disagreed on when Amitabh was on the screen, we would all watch, laugh and get emotional as one, united.

INTRODUCTION

You may wonder why I've taken it upon myself to tell this story. I certainly cannot claim to be his most ardent or greatest fan. I don't think I will ever be able to measure up to the immense adulation, attachment or commitment that I have seen showered upon 'Amitabh' by millions of Indians and other nationalities around the world. I could, however, very modestly admit that I was known to rattle off all his released movies, his co-stars, and directors at the slightest provocation. My most impressive ability was to look at a single screenshot of one his films and be able to name it. To this day, I hold much of that information in my grey cells. My awe for 'Amitabh' still prevents me from referring to him by name and the reverence I have for him has had me incapable of coming up with a term with which I can comfortably address him.

But although I was not one of his greatest fans, I was certainly one of the fans most affected by his injury. It took me a long, long time to get over his accident and near-death experience. Looking back, the almost two months or so that it lasted, I have just snatches of recollection. Some of it stands out for its impact.

One thing I remember starkly is the state I was in. Deeply immobilized by his accident, hospitalization and the ensuing illnesses, I stopped living my normal life. I was in college, but nothing could make me go to my lectures. When forced to go, I couldn't function normally. I would be in class, but could only offer a blank look. My classmates understood my preoccupation, filling in attendance for me, while I stared out the library window. I was a zombie, absently following my routine, while my mind was constantly following the happenings at Breach Candy Hospital.

You may want to know here:

Did I go and visit him?

Was I one of the thousands that waited outside the hospital every day?

Was I there when he finally walked out of that hospital, back from the jaws of death, a shadow of his original self?

And my answer is No, No and No to all the questions.

I was in such a state of shock and denial, that in my mind all this was not happening for real. If I didn't go and wait outside the hospital, all this might just turn out to be a horrible dream. I could not bring myself to face the happenings of those days where the mind would go through sadness, disbelief, hope, despair, joy, so many emotions.

It was only after the ordeal was over and Amitabh was discharged from the hospital that the world saw how traumatic those days were, not only for the star and his family but for millions of fans all over India.

Though I was not present outside the hospital, I was like a stricken puppy, faithfully following his fateful accident and the accompanying complications through any means available. There was no Google, or Internet and none of the current information excess that we all can so easily access today. At that time, I had to rely on whatever newspaper articles I could lay my hands on, watch the limited news on 'Doordarshan' or tune in to 'All India Radio'!

I held on to each piece of news as it happened.

At first, I started saving the entire newspaper but my family got mad at me. You see, I was an early riser. I would be the first one to read the newspaper at home, then pass it on to my mum & dad. But if the paper had any article on Him, I would hide the entire paper and the blame would fall on the 'newspaperwallah' for missing our delivery. Well, that trick didn't last for long. My mum noticed that my study books drawer was bulging and wouldn't fully close. So there I was, sheepish & guilty, but soon forgiven in the light of my passion and affection for this man.

So the next step for me was to keep cuttings of the articles. These cuttings were stored between pages of my drawing book. I would take great comfort in reading about him, so I started to number the articles so I wouldn't get mixed up. Some of them didn't have dates on them at all, unlike articles today. Once, my sister spied on me reading small pieces of newspaper and told my mum. I'd like to add here that I usually kept most things from her since I thought she was a generation younger than me (she is five years younger than me). I also have a brother, the youngest, and by my earlier yardstick, he became two generations younger so he was forbidden from even looking at any of my stuff, leave alone touching it. He was threatened with a week of no Hindi-movie songs or TV if he ever did so and since we had only one 'Cassette tape player and TV', I dominated the 'operating part'. In today's world, we wouldn't even dream of sharing our music or TV, but those were different days, of one electronic gadget per family.

I was then supposed to share my cuttings with them both since whatever I did, they had to do (it's a sibling thing). But this being my lifeline, my oxygen to keep me going, I couldn't share the newspaper pieces with her, so she did the next best thing. She flicked some of the cuttings to spite me and boy, did that make me angry!!!

There was a big verbal and physical duel but luckily my mum intervened (as always). To calm me down, she came up with a brilliant suggestion; - "Why don't you make this your memory book. Then you can look at it whenever and wherever you want and later when you are in a more amicable and generous mood, you can share it with your sister and your friends?"

This seemed a very sensible and workable thing to do, so I got started. It didn't take me very long and at the end, I had my memory book, to go through umpteen number of times during the day, at my convenience, and to share, if I felt like (which wasn't till much later). Once he was back in action, I could proudly show it off, to whoever was interested.

Years passed by, my life took a lot of twists and turns and I moved countries: from India to the USA, then to Australia, then to the USA and back to Australia, following his screen presence and happenings throughout this time.

Much later, in 2011, a friend invited me to the filming of an episode of his show, 'Kaun Banega Crorepati'. I couldn't believe my luck!! I would actually be seeing my idol for real, instead of on screen. It would be my very first 'up, close and personal' meeting with my hero, my star!

During the filming, I sat by the side of the stage and watched him work, completely enthralled by this man who I had loved for so long. After filming was complete, he took the time to speak with all of us. For me, it was an unforgettable experience that proved yet again how humble, caring and charismatic he still is. After filming, the channel was kind enough to send me the photo we shared.

AMITABH -THE PHENOMENON
The Icon. The Legend. The Actor. The Superstar

Meet the biggest movie star in the world: Mr. Amitabh Bachchan.

Bollywood has seen a number of superstars, but this man remains the one and only megastar. He is the face that four generations of India can recognize. He doesn't need an introduction; he is a brand unto himself. Despite his age (he will be 76 in October 2018), he's still a big force to be reckoned with and a very important part of Bollywood. At an age where many others in the industry would think about retirement, he's still always on his feet, busier than ever, entering his 50th year of "being in films and show business". His impressive back catalogue of stellar performances has won him many hearts, and he'll continue to do so for years to come. But none of these facts can fully express the adoration that this man earns from his fans.

So how can I truly paint a picture of his stature to the uninitiated?

It is not easy to explain the Amitabh Bachchan phenomenon to Indian teenagers who missed out on the superstar's golden days in the 1970s and 1980s, let alone to those unfamiliar with Indian films or Bollywood. An entire generation grew up idolizing Amitabh, copying his hairstyle, his walk, and even his rich baritone.

Maybe I could say that the man possesses the combined screen presence of Sean Connery, Harrison Ford, and George Clooney?

Or the rugged charm and potent aggression of Marlon Brando, Robert De Niro, and Clint Eastwood?

1

Or that he has millions of followers on Social Media?

Or that he has a separate Wikipedia page devoted only to the awards he has won?

Or maybe I should pose a question: how many other actors could suffer a serious injury, and have fans offering sacrifices of their limbs to save his?

Or how many other actors would inspire one man to walk 300 miles backwards in divine supplication to heal his injury?

Amitabh Bachchan (or Big B, as he is fondly referred to) is in a league of his own. With his chestnut hair, white goatee and deep-set, intense eyes behind his glasses, he is relentlessly humble. He will tell you it was all a happy accident; that his success was due to the writers and directors and nothing to do with him. But this humility obscures the truth. Amitabh Bachchan, the artiste, puts his heart and soul into the role and is one of the most punctual and impressive stars on set. Throughout his career, Amitabh has worked not only with most senior directors but also new talent with equal ease. It's a fact that he currently works with directors who grew up worshipping him.

The Man: For the Masses and Classes

In the 1970s and 1980s, India was a society full of injustices, criminality, and corruption. Rapid industrialization brought a lot of prosperity to the country but also created the big divide. The rich soared while the common man floundered. As the population drifted towards the big cities, slums became commonplace, and with them, slum lords and gang leaders. The average family man felt unsafe and abandoned, with little clue as to how he could physically defend himself and his family in an emergency situation. Increasing affluence and consumerism made smuggling a well-paying business and the kingpins among smugglers were even accepted in society. The law offered little protection and often citizens felt the need to find protection from the law itself.

Through his characters, Amitabh was a man for the underdog. He showed how social pressures could force a perfectly innocent man to become a smuggler or lawbreaker. His movies were always about 'fight for your right' and a 'fight to the finish'. A victory or 'Vijay' for the powerless and a triumph of justice. When Amitabh delivered those punches on screen, the average viewer saw him as an ally. We all related to Amitabh, picturing ourselves as the ones who were delivering those blows. But these weren't battles of our own. They were the battles of the masses.

In all his films, Amitabh's character stood up for the ordinary man against the injustices of the establishment. This earned him instant affiliation with those who were struggling to cope with poverty. Such was his popularity that during this period, Amitabh would be filming up to 12 movies simultaneously. In some, he played double roles. In one film, he even portrayed a father and both of his sons. He had a mesmerizing presence: he made you believe that one man was genuinely capable of changing the world.

In our highly romance-oriented commercial cinema, a star's stature gets its strength from an aura they project. These images that are perceived or impressions that are formed are built around the quixotic. A chivalrous, romantic concept of the ideal man for the female audience and for the male audience, an ideal concept of masculinity to which they can aspire. Amitabh Bachchan fulfilled this important role for both. For the female audience, he provided an identity figure around which dreams could be woven and around which millions of girls could build their fantasies. But this romantic perception was not that of a goody-goody image of the lover boy. It was one where his physical attributes played a major part. The tall frame, consistently flattered in low angle shots, the silent gaze conveying smoldering passion, the intense squint promising reserves of sadistic rage and the voice: deep, resolute and vibrant.

And this is how Amitabh became an influencer:

For women, their invincible hero!

For men, their messiah!

The Persistent, Motivated Self-starter

One would think that the past of a star would be just as glamorous and tinsel-colored as his future. But Amitabh Bachchan came to the screen enveloped in the mist of anonymity. He was scoffed at due to his tall, gawky stature. After a series of rejections, both in the film world and outside of it, Amitabh refused to give up hope. The entire industry should be grateful for that today. He was even turned down for an announcer role by All India Radio because, believe it or not, his voice was 'not right'. He was then refused the job of a junior executive in a consumer goods firm in Delhi. Following this, he joined the crowd of young hopefuls on trams, clutching his testimonials and wearing the 'ubiquitous suits of anonymous executives' in Calcutta. For a while, he worked as a shipping agent. This involved, in his own words, "drinking a lot of beer and doing really nothing much." After searching for work in all possible places, he headed to Bombay, the city of dreams and opportunity, as his heart was still set on becoming an actor and this was his 'now or never' moment.

Even here, there were plenty of knocks on doors, many turn-offs and no work in the big tough city. Things were pretty rough with no money and no support that Amitabh even spent many nights on Marine Drive, sleeping on a bench with nowhere to go.

Dejected, he almost decided to give up on his dream. But he persisted with his efforts, and it was then he got his first break with the movie *Saat Hindustani* (1969) for which he even won the national award. However, things didn't ease up immediately after getting into films. He was made to wait on sets for unreasonable lengths of time. He was never given any encouragement and to get his next role he had to struggle for another two years. Then came *Anand* (1971) followed by *Zanjeer* (1973), which changed his life forever.

While this is not meant to be a rags-to-riches story, it certainly serves as a great example of persistence, of motivation in the face of adversity and rejection. It offers us insight into the struggle that one goes through to get a decent break in the film industry. It should serve as an inspiration (and warning) to new aspirants who naively wish for fame and instant success in the film industry to fall into their lap. The tall, gawky newcomer with the extra-long legs soon became the yardstick that would out-measure the other stars.

"I'm a self-made man. I took nobody's help. I struggled for every penny I've earned. Someone once told me, if you learn to play golf and sip beer in the afternoon you can land yourself a nice, firm job in Calcutta. So I put on my raw silk jacket and went from office to office putting on my best English accent, and got a job with Bird and Co. My first salary was Rs. 470 a month. When I saw this ad in the papers for new talent, my brother, Bunty took a box camera picture of mine outside the Victoria Memorial and we sent it to a studio. K.A. Abbas signed me up for my first picture, Saat Hindustani, for which I got Rs. 3,000. This is how I started.

A big takeaway from this story also relates to body image and body shaming attitudes that are so prevalent today. Constant exposure to idealized media images of flawless human perfection can keep us aware of our own physical shortcomings. Most people see at least one part or aspect of their physical appearance that they don't like. When this body image becomes confused with personality and self-esteem, it becomes a big limiting factor for moving forward in life and in achieving our life goals.

A person's self-worth is so much higher and different than how one sees, thinks and feels about their physical appearance. The physical is only a very small part of who the person is. Just imagine, if Amitabh had to listen to and give in to all those naysayers, his acting career would have stopped before he could even get started. There were many who dissuaded him from considering acting because of his voice, long legs, non-conventional looks and non-chocolate hero image, but he held on to his self-belief, his confidence. He persisted and did not give up on his dream.

Many have commented how Amitabh's career is a tale of luck added to good fortune, calling it a series of timely coincidences. With legendary modesty, Amitabh refuses to take any credit for himself. But let's face it: even if he was more fortunate than the others, he has worked very hard to get where he is. He has been a professional to work with, the perfect 'Director's Actor'. As far as work is concerned, none of his directors ever said a word against him. He is always on time, always addresses directors as Sir or Madam, and has reportedly never refused or complained about a scene, no matter what the hardship.

Amitabh never bragged about himself. But yes, he was confident from the start. During the early 70s, he was going through a bad patch. None of his movies were doing well. A filmmaker at a meeting with Amitabh said, "If this film doesn't work, I will be out of business." Amitabh looked at him and said, "I've been doing second, third and fourth leads in films for a while. I'm going through a rough patch. But I know I'll bounce back. I will occupy the top slot and stay there."

It was the early 80s that were marked by great heights and new records for Amitabh's career as he touched the peak of his legend and power. He was now the complete entertainer, the one man industry who could conjure successes out of the most unlikely of films. By this time he had worked in more than 100 films, many of which made cinematic history.

Within a decade, he made it big and the world saw. And it was his sheer confidence that catapulted him to the height of success - an artiste who braved and survived the winds of change.

Charismatic

'Charisma' is defined as the power to inspire devotion and enthusiasm. In ancient Greek, it meant the gift of grace or favor. In Hollywood terms, it translates to the kind of box office appeal that earns some actors more than $US20 million a film. In the world of Bollywood, it boils down to the spectacular success of an individual. It's the ability to hold sway over millions of people for decades, unfailingly answering to their need for an icon and living up to their expectations. Charisma is the stuff that idols are made of.

AMITABH -THE PHENOMENON

What was behind Amitabh Bachchan's charisma?

Amitabh radiates a self-confidence other people find inspiring and intriguing. But Amitabh's charisma is about more than simply being intriguing or physically attractive. Watching him on screen, audiences feel that they have a friend up there willing and able to fight their battles with his bare fists. Someone smart, clever and strong enough to protect them from life's unfairness.

Amitabh represented an anti-establishment attitude, which was typical of the world at the time. That world was marked by strife, dissent, and disrespect towards all institutions. Music and other popular arts were changing. Amitabh helped change filmmaking in our country, giving the once lowly 'stunt film' a new dimension. Gave it Power and Cult status.

He was the unlikeliest of candidates for stardom: A poet's son, a tall, awkward figure, a rank outsider as it were. On getting his first roles, he showed no inclination to change his name into a hopefully more romantic one—an old custom in Bollywood. And he showed no interest in developing a second front for the sake of his career, a heightened, artificial 'image' presented for public consumption, another old custom. He remained himself. He didn't even seem to mind public discussion of his asthma or the dreaded myasthenia gravis that he contracted after his accident. And all of this was in an industry where, even today, leading stars barely permit an occasional photograph of themselves with their prescription glasses on.

The only irony was that Amitabh, the anti-authority figure of the screen, was in time transformed into an establishment figure himself. It was his turn to be chipped away at, much to his irritation, and the film gossip press was doing it. As the gossip mills were being fueled by stories, controversies, Amitabh reacted by cutting himself off from the press and turning cold and indifferent. But in real life, he was the suave, well-mannered, well-spoken, well-read debonair gentleman- a committed professional whose punctuality and perfectionism became traits to emulate.

All this added to his Charisma and made him irresistible!!

The One Man Industry

So total was Amitabh Bachchan's dominance of the movie scene in the 1970s and 1980s that the French director François Truffaut called him a "One-Man Industry". Such was the euphoria of his superstardom that in the biggest movie industry in the world, Amitabh was the only man who could claim this title for more than one and a half decades. For anyone who may not know what a one-actor movie was like, here is the best example. 'The plot is ridiculous, and really makes no sense. It's full of clichéd situations, hackneyed lines, melodrama, comedy... you name it! But then you had Amitabh Bachchan in the film. And that made all the difference. It was a guaranteed hit.'

The achievements of Amitabh are unimaginable. I do not have the space here to run through all the best moments from his career. But I'll try.

Sholay and *Deewar,* two of the greatest commercial films in Indian history were both released in 1975. This is the year the world was introduced to Amitabh's superstardom. For the next few years, everything he touched turned into gold. Even his less popular films generated more attention, and often more revenue, than the hit films of other stars.

It took the next two years to consolidate Amitabh's super-stardom status as Manmohan Desai and Prakash Mehra competed with each other to produce one roaring hit after another. Of the six Amitabh films released in 1977, all introduced a new Amitabh to the audiences. Though Amitabh shared the limelight with other heroes, he stole scenes with his charisma, even if the roles remained scrupulously equal. In that year, four films became mega-successes.

In October 1978, in that one month, he delivered four commercial successes in a row. The films were released back-to-back and went on to become super hits: *Muqaddar Ka Sikander, Kasme Vaade, Don* and *Trishul.* In two of these four films Amitabh played a double role, so in fact, there were six different characters that he portrayed.

As the years rolled into the 1980s, specifically 1982, it reached a stage when it seemed that Amitabh could do anything and get away with it. With *Namak Halal,* Amitabh illustrated his command and maturity. Everyone in the movie turns in a good performance, but our megastar overshadows them with his towering presence. Without him, this movie would have been a non-starter. Amitabh's performance was brilliant, on all counts, and an otherwise silly film became ridiculously funny.

It became clear to all that Amitabh represented not just the rise of a great talent but also a sure-shot box-office success. Hits followed hits over the next few years, as even minor films became major successes.

As it Happened

Saturday, 24th July 1982, Day Zero

The superstar on the sets of *Coolie*, deep in thought, waiting for his shot.

The superstar on the sets of *Coolie* where he was seriously injured

Amitabh Bachchan was in Bangalore shooting Manmohan Desai's film *Coolie*.

It was Saturday. For the cast and crew, it was just another day on the sets being 'on location', doing set-ups for their next shot. It had been a week of long days for everyone, keeping up with the hours and momentum required for the 'fight scenes'. Everyone was looking forward to ending the week on a high note, shooting a fight scene between Amitabh Bachchan and his new co-star Puneet Issar.

In this movie, Amitabh plays a railway porter, supported by a cast of Rishi Kapoor, Rati Agnihotri, Kader Khan, Waheeda Rehman, Suresh Oberoi and Puneet Issar. In the director's chair was Mr. Manmohan Desai, the biggest showman in Bollywood, and he was directing his favorite actor Amitabh. Theirs was a winning combination and this pair had churned out a few blockbusters since working together. It was no secret that Manmohan Desai had discovered his alter ego with Amitabh Bachchan. They shared a close rapport, both on and off screen, allowing Amitabh limitless improvisation and creative freedom. Together they gave the audience quintessential Bollywood entertainers. 'Coolie' as their new action, comedy film was expected to follow the same path.

The scene was set for this fight sequence being filmed at Bangalore city's Jnana Bharati University campus. The university library had been rearranged to resemble the inside of a bank and the script called for the villain, played by Puneet Issar, to get into a fight with Amitabh. It was Puneet's first day on the set and his first shot. Amitabh and Puneet were supposed to trade punches in a well-rehearsed action sequence.

And then tragedy struck.

While landing on a table, Amitabh mistimed his jump, hitting the corner of the table, instead of landing on top of it as he was meant to. His lower abdomen came into painful contact with the edge of the table.

At first, nobody realized anything had gone wrong. Desai applauded the star's realistic acting but stopped when he and the rest of the crew realized that something was seriously wrong. In excruciating pain, Amitabh staggered out of the set and onto the lawns. At first, the crew members thought he was faking but soon realized he wasn't. Amitabh, according to eye-witness reports, stood up, took two steps rubbing his stomach and then crumpled to the floor, his face in pain.

Thinking that this was a temporary and minor injury, Amitabh was rushed back to the West End Hotel suite that he had occupied for the past two weeks. When the pain failed to subside over the next few hours, a doctor who was a family acquaintance was called in to examine the star. The doctor felt it was nothing serious and prescribed some painkillers. By then it was around 8 p.m., almost five hours since the incident had taken place, and his condition seemed to have worsened. Amitabh's wife Jaya Bachchan, who had flown into Bangalore with their two children to spend the Eid holiday with her husband, was becoming increasingly anxious. She later told doctors that he had spent the first night in extreme agony.

Sunday, 25th July 1982, Day One

The next morning, on Sunday, Amitabh's personal physician, Dr. K. M. Shah, flew down from Bombay in reply to an urgent SOS. Amitabh was still obviously in excruciating agony. Dr. Shah expressed his concern, which was enough to rush the star to St. Philomena's hospital for an X-ray and admittance. A senior surgeon examined him and stated that "There is no cause for alarm". The X-rays failed to show any serious injury and a physical examination only revealed a tender spot in his abdomen but little else.

Monday, 26th July 1982, Day Two

Article # 1. Amitabh hurt

It was a full 48 hours before the media or the general public knew or had even heard about the accident. None, except for his family and officials, present there had any inkling of what was going on. There was a small article reported on one of the inside pages referring to Amitabh's accident as 'an incident'. Today, everybody feeds on celebrity status and there is an overload, an amassing of information about the here and now. News goes around in a loop via instant tweets and feeds going viral across the globe.

But those were different times. We have to bear in mind, this was the 1980s. There was none of the scrutiny that celebrities face today. Nor were there this multitude of mobile satellite vans zooming in on news and incidents as they happen. Indian cinema did not get a mention in the newspapers. This medium was reserved only for 'serious stuff'. It was all about business affairs, corporate news, financial deals, socio-economic happenings and World news. Only these made headlines and were accorded the importance of the first few pages. Those days there were very few television channels, no Google or YouTube, no way of finding out much about a film personality except in film magazines, and even then days after the fact.

It was already Monday, two days since he was hurt. Amitabh showed no signs of improvement, though he was fully conscious. The hospital performed another X-ray, which again failed to reveal any serious complications.

The medical bulletin issued by the hospital stated that the star was "improving". But the fact was, two days of untreated intestinal leakage had resulted in severe internal infection and peritonitis, the inflammation of the abdominal lining. The rupture of the large intestine had spilt toxic faecal contents into Amitabh's abdomen resulting in septicemia.

All of this was only discovered later. However, Dr. Shah instinctively felt that something was seriously wrong and he was in a quandary. He didn't know whether flying the star to

Bombay would aggravate the injury. He consulted Jaya and they booked seats for a flight that evening.

By the evening, however, Amitabh's condition had deteriorated markedly and the seats were cancelled. Though it had been two days since the incident, the outside world, including the media, remained in the dark. On instructions from the star's family, the hospital had kept a tight-lipped silence on Amitabh's condition except for terse words of encouragement that turned out to be hopelessly false.

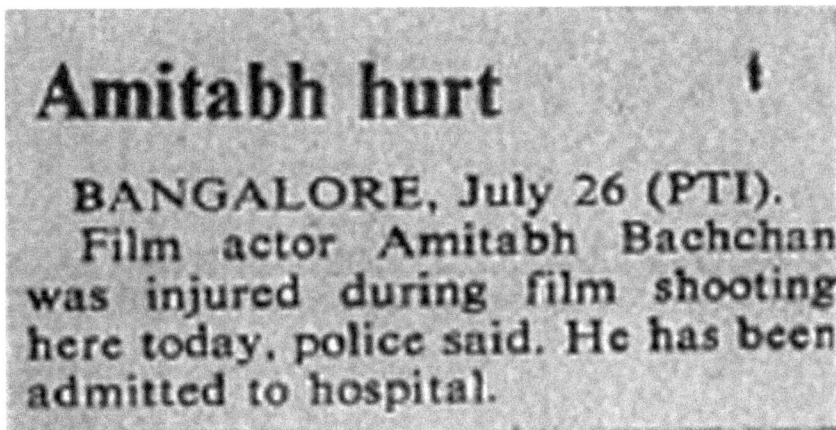

Amitabh hurt

BANGALORE, July 26 (PTI).
Film actor Amitabh Bachchan was injured during film shooting here today, police said. He has been admitted to hospital.

Tuesday, 27th July 1982, Day Three

Article # 2. Amitabh operated upon

It was now almost 72 hours since Amitabh was hurt. It was not evident at that time but this delay was getting deadlier by the minute. Nobody could see or was even aware that by the minute, the perforated intestinal wall was slowly leaking poisonous wastes into the internal organs and spreading infection throughout the body.

On the surface, it seemed that there was action all around and 'things' were happening. But in reality, it lacked the urgency and decisiveness this situation warranted. The hesitation on part of everyone present, though undesirable was understandable as Amitabh was classed under what was called as 'The VIP Syndrome', a term used notoriously within the medical profession. The doctors are hesitant to involve themselves in any procedure fearing repercussions due to sensitivity of the patient's fame and reputation.

Thankfully, as the day progressed, 'things' started moving when anxious messages from Rajiv Gandhi, who was in the USA at that time, arrived and Chief Minister Gundu Rao and senior state officials got into the act. Dr. Shah took advantage of this sudden air of urgency and called in Dr. H.S. Bhatt, one of the leading urologists in the country to examine Amitabh.

This time, however, Dr. Bhatt's diagnosis was brisk and decisive; Amitabh required an immediate operation. Even then, there was some agonizing delay over the possibility of flying in surgeons from Bombay. But by now Amitabh's condition was too serious for the 12-hour delay that this would have entailed. He was running a high fever, vomiting repeatedly and by 2:30 that afternoon his heartbeat had run to 180 as against the normal 72. He had also slipped into a coma.

The surgery took place in limited facilities, and the operation took a total of three hours but with the warning that the stomach would rupture again and another surgery would be needed soon. Waiting anxiously outside the operation theatre were Amitabh's wife Jaya, his mother Teji, his brother Ajitabh and film producer Yash Johar.

Before the operation ended, three specialists from Bombay had flown in to observe the final stages. They were Dr. M.K. Gandhi, chief of cardiology, Dr. Sharad Shah, a gastroenterologist, and Dr. Shirish K. Bhansali, a surgeon specializing in hepato-pancreo-biliary surgery.

By now, the word had spread and pools of anxious fans had gathered outside the hospital, in spite of pounding rain. The crucial vigil had begun. The first 24 hours are the most vital hours after any major operation and it was now a question of waiting, of hope and prayer.

Amitabh operated upon

BANGALORE, July 27 (PTI).
Film star Amitabh Bachchan today underwent surgery for a reported intestinal rupture sustained during the shooting of a fight sequence here yesterday.

His actress-wife, jaya Bhaduri, who waited anxiously in the corridor outside the operation theatre while the surgery was going on, told PTI later that the doctors had told her that her husband was progressing.

Hospital sources said it had earlier been decided to shift Mr. Bachchan to Bombay this afternoon. But as his condition turned a "little serious", the doctors decided to operate.

The actor reportedly received the injury when he dived on to a table after a 'villain' in the film hit him in the stomach.

Hospital sources said Mr. Bachchan had regained consciousness after the operation. He would be under observation for the next 24 hours.

Wednesday, 28th July 1982, Day Four

Article # 3. Amitabh under close watch

After the operation, Amitabh was under close supervision. The doctors gave him only a 50% chance of survival. The next morning, however, ushered in further complications. His lungs had deteriorated, and doctors suspected he was suffering from pneumonia. The actor was also becoming increasingly delirious.

The doctors would have liked to examine his chest cavity and lungs through a bronchoscope. They debated the feasibility of doing so, as it amounted to a great risk at that stage of Amitabh's struggle for survival. The decision was put off till later as Amitabh's life still hung by a very slender thread.

In today's times, an immediate detection of the injury would have been a matter of some scans and the medical procedure would not have been so alarming. But this was in the early 80s. And Bangalore in 1982 was not the Bengaluru of today. Medical facilities were limited and not as sophisticated as the situation demanded. A portable x-ray machine was used to diagnose which revealed an image of a cloud above the diaphragm but was so light that it did not draw the attention of the doctors. Apparently this was an indication that there had been a rupture in the intestine and the gases had collected, but unfortunately, it escaped the attention of everyone present.

The seventy-two hours that elapsed between getting hurt and surgery being performed turned out to be life-threatening in those circumstances as it allowed toxic wastes to enter the bloodstream and permeated through into the stomach, affecting all vital organs.

Amitabh under close watch

BANGALORE, July 28 (UNI).

Hindi film hero Amitabh Bachchan who underwent a laparotomy (incision into the abdominal cavity), described by doctors as a major surgery, is reported to be getting better this evening.

Amitabh sustained an internal injury during the shooting of a fight sequence for a film.

The star was now under sedation and he was being kept on under a close 24-hour observation.

The hospital authorities said Amitabh was given blood this evening and his condition was much better compared to yesterday.

Medical specialists who arrived here from Bombay last night are still here to deal with any emergency that may crop up.

The laporotomy operation was performed by doctors last evening when Bachchan's condition became serious as a result of the swelling of the membranes surrounding the viscera. The star's abdominal cavity was pierced when he fell onto a sharp edged steel table during a fight sequence.

Prime Minister Indira Gandhi and Mr. Rajiv Gandhi, MP have expressed concern over the health of Amitabh Bachchan.

Thursday, 29th July 1982 to Sunday 1st August 1982, Day Five, Six, Seven and Eight

Article # 4 and Article # 5
Amitabh being shifted to Bombay, Amitabh 'out of danger'

Amitabh's condition was getting worse as the doctors were now concerned about his kidneys. On that Thursday night, they made the decision to fly him to Bombay. The journey was kept a strict secret due to the increasing number of well-wishers, visitors, political personalities and media turning his illness into a media circus. By Friday morning, Amitabh's condition had improved, although he had developed slight jaundice. Doctors decided to fly him out on the evening Airbus flight rather than a chartered flight to avoid a bumpy ride. The Bombay airbus flight was three hours late and by the time three rows of seats had been removed to accommodate the mini-intensive care unit, it was well past midnight before the plane took off.

Director Manmohan Desai made immediate arrangements to fly his injured star to Bombay. In a typical film fashion, Amitabh's transfer from the hospital was conducted like a top secret operation. While the plethora of reporters and photographers waited in ambush at the front door, Amitabh was spirited out on a stretcher through the rear door and into a waiting ambulance. A police escort accompanied the cavalcade to the airport and at 40 minutes past midnight, the plane took off for Bombay in a rescue mission to save the actor's life. En route, Amitabh was barely conscious and could not speak. The plane landed at Bombay's Santa Cruz airport where director Yash Chopra had organized an ambulance to take him straight to Breach Candy Hospital.

Once Amitabh arrived in Bombay, the team of doctors got into action in the intensive care unit. Manmohan Desai, along with a number of other producers including Yash Chopra, Yash Johar, and Prakash Mehra, kept a constant vigil outside the hospital, providing support to Amitabh's family.

Amitabh being 4· shifted to Bombay

Express News Service

BANGALORE, July 30.
Hindi film star Amitabh Bach-chan, who was being treated at the St. Philomina's Hospital here during the last five days, is being shifted to the Breach Candy Hospital in Bombay tonight. He will be taken in an airbus flight.

UNI adds: Dr. C. D. Jacob, Medical Superintendent of the Saint Philomina Hospital, said Bachchan was better and his all-important health parameters were "doing fairly well". Since the platellet factor of the blood had been found "deficient", the team decided not to take any risks, he said. Bachchan was given a platellet transfusion this morning

Amitabh 'out 5· of danger'

By A Staff Reporter

Superstar Amitabh Bachchan was declared 'out of danger' on Sunday by doctors attending him at the Breach Candy Hospital.

The actor, however, continues to be in the intensive care unit and under observation. His condition gave anxious moments to the team of doctors attending on him on Saturday.

A close relative said Amitabh was "fast improving." He was said to be speaking to family members and close friends, who were allowed to meet him.

A large number of admirers came to the hospital to enquire about the health of their idol. But, none was allowed to meet him.

Amitabh underwent surgery at Bangalore in the Saint Philomena's hospital on Tuesday for a ruptured intestine suffered during the shooting of the film "Coolie." A team of eminent doctors had accompanied him on the flight to Bombay.

21

Monday, 2nd August 1982, Day Nine

Amitabh had to undergo a second major operation soon after he arrived at Breach Candy for a burst abdomen when stitches administered in Bangalore gave way. Amitabh's second operation in Bombay turned into an eight-hour battle for life. At the end of it, he was still very much in a critical condition.

"I went into almost a haze and a coma-like situation. Within five days of coming into Breach Candy, I had another surgery and didn't come out of that one for a very very long time and I was clinically dead for a couple of minutes. Then Dr. Wadia, who looked after me and is an absolute life-saver, just said "I'm going to take a last chance" and he started pumping cortisone injections into me one after another almost, 40 ampules of it, with the hope that something would happen and then I got revived".

It is not widely known but on this day, Amitabh had slipped into a coma. The operation was over but there was still no sign of life. For almost two minutes, he was declared clinically dead. In a last-ditch measure, the doctors injected adrenaline and cortisone straight into Amitabh's heart. Almost immediately, Jaya Bachchan saw one of his toes move and exclaimed: "Look, he's alive." Amitabh had come back from the deep-end, fighting his way through the jaws of death! It was truly a miracle. And this is how 2nd August became Amitabh Bachchan's second birthday.

The mood was one of despair in the intensive care unit. However, the news the hospital reported was to the contrary. (Refer article for Tuesday, 3rd August, Day Ten) There were reasons for this discrepancy. The authorities didn't give all the information to the press in an attempt to curb the growing hysteria of the public, as well as the surge of crowds outside the hospital. It had become an issue of law and order for the already stretched administration.

Amitabh is better

6.

By A Staff Reporter

The condition of superstar Amitabh Bachchan was "improving" the Breach Candy Hospital authorities said on Monday night.

Amitabh continues to be in the intensive care unit and is under very careful observation, according to the hospital sources.

His condition is getting stabilised and it may take a few days before he would be well enough to be able to move.

Members of his family were with him on Monday and he spoke to them. Visitors were still not allowed to see or meet him.

A large number of the admirers of the matinee idol continue to come to the hospital to enquire about his health.

Chief Minister Babasaheb Bhosale on Monday enquired on telephone about the condition of Amitabh Bachchan and was told that he was progressing.

Amitabh operated upon

By A Staff Reporter

Amitabh Bachchan's condition was reported to be "progressing" by a spokesman of the Breach Candy Hospital on Tuesday night. In the morning his health caused some concern to the doctors attending on him.

This followed an emergency operation on Monday when his condition had suddenly taken a turn for worse. However, Mr. Bachchan regained consciousness on Tuesday morning and doctors attending on him said that he would be alright.

As the superstar's health fluctuated from time to time, his family members, friends, relatives and fans gathered outside the hospital.

A close watch was kept on him by a team of doctors to check any new developments, a source close to the Bachchan family said. Some essential drugs for his treatment, and possibly a doctor, were expected to be flown to Bombay from abroad.

The film actor had been operated in Bangalore last week for an intestinal injury received during the shooting of a fight sequence for the film "Coolie." He had been flown to Bombay on Saturday and admitted to the Breach Candy Hospital.

Security at the hospital is very tight as several of his fans crowd the area, eagerly awaiting news about his health.

Chief Minister Babasaheb Bhosale, along with his wife, visited the Hospital on Monday night, to enquire about the star's health.

Tuesday, 3rd August 1982 and Wednesday, 4th August 1982, Day Ten and Eleven

Article # 6 and Article # 7. Amitabh is better, Amitabh operated upon

The Hospital authorities were being non-committal with a status of "Amitabh is improving and his condition is getting stabilized".

The Chief Minister was given the same news as were all the other admirers who would come to enquire about the star's health. However, the Chief Minister with his wife visited Amitabh on Monday night

On Monday, Amitabh and his family had been through a harrowing time, fighting for his life and the hospital authorities had adopted a very sensible approach in maintaining order and calm as a huge crowd waited outside the hospital, eager for news about the star's health.

India held its breath as Amitabh battled for his life.

The mood of the crowds waiting patiently outside the hospital was one of hope. There were prayers being offered in temples, mosques, and churches throughout the country. The entire nation came together as one, transcending boundaries of caste, creed, religion, age, and gender. The collective power of prayers, the sentiment of unity in diversity, all that Amitabh portrayed through his movies, now became a reality.

The mood in the hospital was sombre, but it was hardly one of defeat. Doctors felt that he had crossed the hump and the worst was over. By this time, Amitabh had regained consciousness and his team of doctors were positive that he would become alright. Amitabh's glassed-off booth in the intensive care unit was a maze of blipping machines and intricate life-support systems. Tubes leading to his abdomen fed antibiotics directly onto the site of the infection while others were required to flush it out twice daily. A tracheal tube had been inserted in his throat to help him breathe since the star's asthmatic tendency put an additional strain on his lungs. A respirator was strapped to his chest to ensure regular air supply and a string of monitors wired to other parts of his body were constantly checking for unforeseen complications.

Rajiv dashes to see Amitabh

By A Staff Reporter

Mr. Rajiv Gandhi, M.P., arrived in Bombay at midnight by a British Airways flight. Mr. Gandhi had cut short his US visit to see Amitabh Bachchan. Rajiv Gandhi wasn't accompanied by any family members.

Mr. Gandhi, who was received at the airport by Maharashtra Chief Minister Babasaheb Bhosale and Bombay Regional Congress(I) Committee chief Murali Deora, inquired about the health of Amitabh, who is undergoing treatment in the Breach Candy Hospital in South Bombay.

Mr. Gandhi had been advised by Prime Minister Indira Gandhi to see the film star.

Later he drove with Mr. Bhosale and Mr. Deora to Raj Bhavan. He is expected to visit the hospital tomorrow morning.

The condition of Amitabh Bachchan, who had undergone an emergency operation on Monday at the Breach Candy Hospital, was said to be "better."

The film actor was "progressing" in the intensive care unit, the doctors attending on him said tonight.

His health had caused anxiety after the emergency operation on Monday and he had regained consciousness on Tuesday.

Wednesday, 4th August 1982, Day Eleven

Article # 8. Rajiv dashes to see Amitabh

Rajiv Gandhi cut short his USA trip and air-dashed to Bombay to visit his friend, drove straight to the hospital from the airport at midnight. Amitabh was under heavy sedation and barely conscious. Rajiv visited the hospital and spent time with the family being their moral support through this ordeal. The next day, on Thursday morning, he spoke at length with the doctors attending Amitabh. At this point Amitabh was still in intensive care and barely conscious. By Thursday evening, Amitabh had regained consciousness and Rajiv could spend some time with Amitabh before leaving that night.

Amitabh and Rajiv's friendship went a long way back. They first met when Amitabh was four and Rajiv only two years old at a fancy dress party at the Bachchans residence in Allahabad. As they grew up, their school holidays fell around the same months and they would hang out and go swimming every day.

The friendship continued even after school when Rajiv went to study at Cambridge, while Amitabh continued in India. Their friendship deepened when Amitabh and his family lent moral support to Rajiv during his marriage with Sonia who had arrived from Italy. Amitabh's mother Teji played the part of the bride's mother and Sonia stayed with the Bachchans a couple of weeks before the wedding. In Indian tradition, the bride-to-be does not stay at her in-laws' house prior to the wedding. The Bachchan family hosted Sonia and her family at their Willingdon Crescent House and helped her learn Indian traditions.

Even after Amitabh became a star, Rajiv would visit him on sets and almost unobtrusively wait patiently outside, till Amitabh completed his shoot. Amitabh would reveal to friends that Rajiv shied away from using his family name or connections for fear that it would create a distance between him and other people and influence normal interactions. In fact, Amitabh said, Rajiv exposed him to avant-garde cinema at a young age through the European films. Rajiv, his brother Sanjay and Amitabh would attend screenings of Czech, Russian and Polish films, often with anti-war messages, at the Gandhi family residence.

Mr. Rajiv Gandhi, who airdashed to Bombay late on Wednesday to see Amitabh Bachchan, coming out of the Breach Candy Hospital after being with the superstar for over 90 minutes on Thursday morning. On extreme right is BRCC(I) President Murli Deora and between them is Dr. Jal Dubash of the Hospital.

Thursday, 5th August 1982, Day Twelve

Article # 9. Amitabh recovering (as transcribed from the article)

Superstar of the Hindi screen, Amitabh Bachchan was "recovering" according to Breach Candy hospital authorities on Thursday.

Mr. Rajiv Gandhi, MP, paid a visit in the morning to the hospital and was with Amitabh and his family for nearly an hour. Mr. Gandhi, who arrived in Bombay around midnight of Wednesday drove straight to the hospital to see Amitabh. He had cut short his US trip.

Mr. Gandhi spoke to doctors attending on Amitabh and enquired about his health. The actor continues to be in the intensive care unit of the hospital and on liquid diet. According to one source, Amitabh was still unconscious and the doctors had to introduce a tracheotomy tube to help the actor breathe with greater ease. His condition had "stabilized" despite the fact that the actor had developed a "lung complication".

A source indicated that he was "not conscious" while others suggested that he may be under heavy sedation. The hospital authorities continue to be stiff-lipped. Amitabh is still not out of danger, according to medical sources outside the hospital, though his condition does not suggest immediate anxiety and he seems to be "rallying around"

Amitabh suffered an intestinal rupture during a fight sequence in the film "Coolie" at Bangalore, where he was operated. Later, he was moved to Bombay and underwent an emergency operation on Monday.

Mr. Murli Deora, BRCC (I) accompanied Mr. Gandhi. A Congress (I) source indicated that Prime Minister Indira Gandhi is anxious to know details about Amitabh's condition. Mr. Gandhi spoke to Dr. F. Udwadia, the surgeon, Dr. Jal Dubash, medical advisor to the hospital was among those who received Mr. Gandhi.

The visit of Mr. Gandhi speaks volumes about the close relationship between the Bachchans and the Gandhis. Amitabh has been very close to Rajiv Gandhi and late

Sanjay Gandhi. Only Mrs. Jaya Bachchan and close family members are allowed to enter the hospital room. The second floor of the intensive care unit is out of bounds for all others and strict measures have been taken to ensure that the star is not disturbed.

Mr. Rajiv Gandhi paid a visit to the hospital on Thursday night, his second during the day. He spent some time with Amitabh and members of the family. The hospital authorities in the night described the condition of the film actor as "better" and "stable".

Amitabh recovering

By A Staff Reporter

Superstar of the Hindi screen, Amitabh Bachchan was "recovering" according to Breach Candy hospital authorities on Thursday.

Mr. Rajiv Gandhi, MP, paid a visit in the morning to the hospital and was with Amitabh and his family for nearly an hour. Mr. Gandhi, who arrived in Bombay around midnight of Wednesday drove straight to the hospital to see Amitabh. He had cut short his US trip.

Mr. Gandhi spoke to doctors attending on Amitabh and enquired about his health. The actor continues to be in the intensive care unit of the hospital and on liquid diet.

According to one source, Amitabh was still unconscious and the doctors had to introduce a tracheotomy tube to help the actor breath with greater ease. His condition has "stabilised" desite the fact that the actor had developed a "lung complication".

A source indicated that he was "not conscious" while others suggested that he may be under heavy sedation. The hospital authorities continue to be stiff-lipped.

Amitabh is still not out of danger, according to medical sources outside the hospital, though his condition does not suggest immediate anxiety and he seems to be "rallying round."

Amitabh suffered an intestinal rupture during a fight sequence in the film "Coolie" at Bangalore, where he was operated. Later, he was moved to Bombay and underwent an emergency operation on Monday.

Mr. Murli Deora, BRCC(I) accompanied Mr. Gandhi. A Congress(I) source indicated that Prime Minister Indira Gandhi is anxious to know details about Amitabh's condition. Mr. Gandhi spoke to Dr. T. Udwadia, the surgeon. Dr. Jal Dubash, medical advisor to the hospital was among those who received Mr. Gandhi.

The visit of Mr. Gandhi speaks volumes of the close relationship between the Bachchans and the Gandhis. Amitabh has been very close to Rajiv Gandhi and late Sanjay Gandhi.

Only Mrs. Jaya Bachchan and close family members are allowed to enter the hospital room. The second floor of the intensive care unit is out of bounds for all others and strict measures have been taken to ensure that the star is not disturbed.

Mr. Rajiv Gandhi paid a visit to the hospital on Thursday night, his second during the day. He spent some time with Amitabh and members of his family. The hospital authorities in the night described the condition of the film actor as "better" and "stable".

31

Friday, 6th August 1982, Day Thirteen

Article #10. Amitabh suffers setback (as transcribed from the article)

Amitabh Bachchan "is not entirely out of danger and is under observation", an official statement of the Breach Candy Hospital announced on Friday night.

After Monday's operation, he was extremely critical and his condition worsened due to development of septic shock, the hospital stated. However, he was resuscitated in the Intensive Care Unit later on.

The superstar had weathered most of the post-operative complications and is conscious now, but still requires respiratory support, the statement added. According to the hospital during Monday's operation, the sutures had given away and there was a great deal of pus in the peritoneum. His abdomen had also become worse.

The hospital said that Amitabh was not receiving any visitors except members of his family. His condition had stabilized now, the statement asserted. However, medical sources outside the hospital suggest that it may be a very long journey of recovery for the matinee idol, and may take a few months for him to be on his legs.

The 40-year-old actor is waging a battle for his life, the sources state. All kinds of complications have come in the way of an early cure. The lung complications and peritonitis, and inflammation around portions of the intestines, following the operation, have been added to this troubles. Tracheotomy had to be resorted to help him breathe more freely.

Meanwhile, on Friday morning, Mr. Rajiv Gandhi, once again visited the hospital, before leaving for Delhi. Mr. Gandhi had cut short his US visit and rushed to Bombay.

Amitabh had been seriously injured during the filming of Hindi film "Coolie" at Bangalore on July 26, and had been brought to Bombay for further treatment.

At the Breach Candy Hospital, he is under the medical supervision of Dr. Sharad Shah, Dr. Sharad (sic) Shirish Bhanshali and Dr. Farokh Udwadia.

Amitabh suffers setback

By A Staff Reporter

Amitabh Bachchan "is not entirely out of danger and is under strict observation," an official statement of the Breach Candy Hospital announced on Friday night.

After Monday's operation he was "extremely critical" and his condition worsened due to development of septic shock, the hospital stated. However, he was resuscitated in the Intensive Care Unit later on.

The superstar had weathered most of the post-operative complications and is conscious now, but still requires respiratory support, the statement added.

According to the hospital during Monday's operation, the sutures had given away and there was a great deal of pus in the peritoneum. His abdomen had also become worse.

The hospital said that Amitabh was not receiving any visitors except members of his family. His condition had stabilized now, the statement asserted.

However, medical sources outside the hospital suggest that it may be a very long journey of recovery for the matinee idol, and may take a few months for him to be on his legs.

The 40-year-old actor is waging a battle for his life, the sources state. All kinds of complications have come in the way of an early cure.

The lung complications and peritonitis, and inflammation around portions of the intestines, following the operation, have added to his troubles. Tracheotomy had to be resorted to help him breathe more freely.

Meanwhile, on Friday morning, Mr. Rajiv Gandhi, once again visited the hospital, before leaving for Delhi. Mr. Gandhi had cut short his US visit and rushed to Bombay.

Amitabh had been seriously injured during the filming of Hindi film "Coolie" at Bangalore on July 26, and had been brought to Bombay for further treatment.

At the Breach Candy Hospital, he is under the medical supervision of Dr. Sharad Shah, Dr. Sharad Bhanshali and Dr. Farokh Udwadia.

Saturday, 7th August 1982, Day Fourteen

Article # 11. Amitabh deteriorating

It was now the fifth day after the harrowing ordeal of the eight-hour operation on Monday and the news was not good. Amitabh's condition was deteriorating. The overwhelming public response included prayers in temples and homes with offers to sacrifice limbs to save him. There were long queues of well-wishing fans outside Breach Candy hospital, where Amitabh was struggling, and facing one medical complication after another.

For these millions of movie-goers, the scene was a familiar one. The tall, lanky frame of their matinee idol Amitabh Bachchan draped over a hospital bed while white-coated figures hovered anxiously around. This time, however, there was a critical difference – there were no cameras and this was not a scene. This was life being played out in the intensive care unit (ICU) of Bombay's Breach Candy Hospital and unfortunately, it was tragically real. Amitabh the nearly indestructible superstar who had battled seemingly insurmountable odds in thousands of celluloid frames, was now fighting the most epic and riveting battle of all - for his life.

Little did anyone know at that time, in order to drain Amitabh's stomach of its impurities and the acute peritonitis, a number of holes were made in his stomach to allow them to flow out. They were flat, corrugated like rubber strips that stuck out of the stomach. Much after his recovery, Amitabh could look back at this incident in a lighter vein and comment, "That he now had a mini -golf course on his stomach; he actually counted the holes and they were 18".

Amitabh deteriorating

BOMBAY, Aug. 7. (PTI).

Film star Amitabh Bachchan's condition has deteriorated, hospital sources said here tonight.

"A little pus formation and more infection are having repercussions on other systems," they told PTI.

The resultant complications which developed were causing "anxiety", the sources added.

Sunday, 8th August 1982, Day Fifteen

Article # 12. Mrs. Gandhi coming

Prime Minister, Indira Gandhi will arrive in Bombay on Sunday to see 40-year old superstar Amitabh Bachchan, who is engaged in a life and death struggle in the intensive care unit of the Breach Candy hospital. She will be accompanied by Rajiv Gandhi, M.P., and his wife Sonia Gandhi.

According to available information, Mrs. Gandhi is flying to Bombay specifically to see Amitabh. This is purely a personal and private visit, it is stated. Her plane will land at Bombay airport at about 10.45 am. She will be taken from the airport to the Breach Candy hospital straightaway.

The Prime Minister of India, Mrs. Indira Gandhi was paying a personal visit as the two families shared a very special friendship going back decades.

Amitabh was the first friend Sonia Gandhi made in India. Throughout their friendship, she affectionately addressed him as Amit and he was the one who received her at Delhi's Palam Airport on the morning of 13th January 1968, when she flew in to be married to Rajiv. During this period, Sonia stayed at Amitabh's house with his parents. Rajiv's wife Sonia referred to him as her brother and her kids Priyanka and Rahul fondly called Amitabh 'Mamun' (maternal uncle in Avadhi language)

Mrs. Gandhi coming

12

By A Staff Reporter

Prime Minister Indira Gandhi will arrive in Bombay on Sunday to see 40-year-old superstar Amitabh Bachchan, who is engaged in a life and death struggle in the intensive care unit of the Breach Candy Hospital.

Mrs. Indira Gandhi will stay in the city for about four hours. She will be accompanied by Mr. Rajiv Gandhi, M.P., and his wife Sonia Gandhi.

According to available information, Mrs. Gandhi is flying to Bombay specifically to see Amitabh. This is purely a personal and private visit, it is stated.

Her plane will land at the Bombay airport at about 10-45 a.m. She will be taken from the air-port to the Breach Candy Hospital straight. After having a lunch at Sahyadri guest house, she is scheduled to be driven back to the air-port for take off to Delhi.

Chief Minister Babasaheb Bhosale, who is in Delhi, is likely to accompany Mrs. Gandhi.

Though the hospital sources are tight-lipped, and did not issue any bulletin on the condition of Amitabh on Saturday, other sources indicated that the film star was kept under sedation. The robust looking actor has gone pale and oedema has set in the legs. He has been given physiotherapy.

A resort has also been taken to draining the pus from his abdomen. His lung complications, difficulty in breathing, septicaemia and peritonitis (inflammation on the sac around some portions of the intestines) have added up to this troubles.

Sunday, 8th August 1982, Day Fifteen

Article # 13. Complications hold up Amitabh's recovery (as transcribed from the article)

On Saturday evening film star Amitabh Bachchan had much more to worry about than the scar on his throat as a result of the tracheotomy tube being inserted to help him breathe.

Sources close to the hospital said he was suffering from high temperature, raised blood pressure, and there were indications of kidney malfunction as blood urea was also high.

He had developed a pancreatic infection, had four tubes draining pus from the abdomen and had been put on intravenous insulin since his blood sugar had shot up. Dr. Kersi N. Dastur was called urgently in the afternoon from Northcote Nursing Home where he has a clinic, to see the patient since he had operated upon him on Monday. He is reported to have said that Amitabh's condition was not as bad as he had expected.

Meanwhile, crowds continued to clog the Breach Candy Hospital even though the star is not allowed to receive visitors. A staggering number of bouquets kept arriving and a check with the secretary who was keeping a full-fledged register of names revealed that more than 3,000 people had left flowers.

The Prime Minister, Mrs. Indira Gandhi, will arrive here on Sunday for a brief visit, according to official sources. Mrs. Gandhi is likely to call on the film star Amitabh Bachchan. Mrs. Gandhi, who will stay at Raj Bhawan, will return to Delhi at 15:00 hours.

The enormous fan following of Amitabh seems to have crossed the bounds of age, color, caste, and creed. Tina Rajan, an eight-year-old girl from Gulmohar Park where the Bachchans are building a house, moved by Amitabh's illness has offered her blood for transfusion.

In a letter to Jaya, the star's actress wife, Tina, a class four student compares herself to the little squirrel in "The Ramayana" which helped Lord Rama build the bridge at Rameswaram to help him cross to Lanka. "I am prepared on my part to do my little bit to alleviate the sufferings of uncle Amitabh," she said.

PAGE THIRTYTWO   SUNDAY MID-DAY, AUGUST 8, 1982

Complications hold up Amitabh's recovery

By A Staff Reporter

On Saturday evening, film star Amitabh Bachchan had much more to worry about than the scar on his throat as a result of the tracheotomy tube being inserted to help him breathe.

Sources close to the hospital said he was suffering from high temperature, raised blood pressure and there were indications of kidney malfunction as blood urea was also high.

He had developed a pancreatic infection, had four tubes draining pus from the abdomen and had been put on intravenous insulin since his blood sugar had shot up.

Dr. Kersi N. Dastur was called urgently in the afternoon from Northcote Nursing Home where he has a clinic, to see the patient since he had operated upon him on Monday. He is reported to have said that Amitabh's condition was not as bad as he had expected.

The film star was in low spirits, in sharp contrast to the preceding day when he wrote notes to the doctor, asking to be allowed to eat something. He was given a cup of tea and even "remarked" that it was a real luxury! On Saturday he was drowsy and disinclined to communicate. He was also rather depressed.

Meanwhile, crowds continued to clog the Breach Candy Hospital even though the star is not allowed to receive visitors. A staggering number of bouquets kept arriving and a check with the secretary who was keeping a full-fledged register of names revealed that more than 3,000 people had left flowers.

The Prime Minister, Mrs. Indira Gandhi, will arrive here on Sunday on a brief visit, according to official sources.

Mrs. Gandhi is likely to call on the film star Amitabh Bachchan. Mrs. Gandhi, who will stay at Raj Bhuvan, will return to Delhi at 1500 hours.

The enormous fan following of Amitabh seems to have crossed the bonds of age, colour, caste and creed.

Tina Rajan, an eight-year-old girl from Gulmohar Park where the Bachchans are building a house, moved by Amitabh's illness has offered her blood for transfusion.

In a letter to Jaya, the star's actress wife, Tina, a class four student compared herself to the little squirrel in "The Ramayana" which helped Lord Rama build the bridge at Rameswaram to help him cross to Lanka.

"I am prepared on my part to do my little bit to alleviate the sufferings of uncle Amitabh," she said.

Sunday, 8th August 1982, Day Fifteen

Article # 14. Everyone's praying

The nation mourned, and fans thronged temples offering to sacrifice limbs in exchange for their hero's recovery.

It became everyone's business to provide 'expert opinions'. Amitabh's health status, his recovery process, the capabilities of Doctors at Breach Candy, the credibility of fight scenes in movies, all of these became the hot topics of discussion for all and sundry.

There were banners erected in different parts of the city, urging Bombayites to pray for his recovery.

Amitabh's wife, Jaya, walked eight kilometers barefoot from Breach Candy to the Siddhi Vinayak Temple every day to pray for Amitabh's recovery.

A banner on Peddar Road says it all.

Everyone's praying

14.

IT SEEMS impossible to get away from Amitabh Bachchan these days. Everyone is talking most knowledgably about his health, the capabilities of the doctors at Breach Candy, exactly how long he will take to recover and whether his fight seems will ever be credible again.

Someone has gone so far as to put up a massive banner near the New Activity School on Peddar Road, praying for his recovery and urging Bombayites to do the same.

If it is irritating for those who sympathise with Amitabh without going into fits of anxiety about him, it must be absolutely maddening for his own family. Mrs. Jaya Bachchan went to the Siddhi Vinayak temple at Prabhadevi to perform puja for the speedy recovery of her husband recently and the mob almost became uncontrollable. She said her prayers in undue haste and left in disgust.

Prime Minister Indira Gandhi caught in an emotional pose with Mrs. Teji Bachchan, mother of Amitabh, at the Breach Candy Hospital on Sunday morning, Mrs. Gandhi was with the superstar at the Hospital for some time.

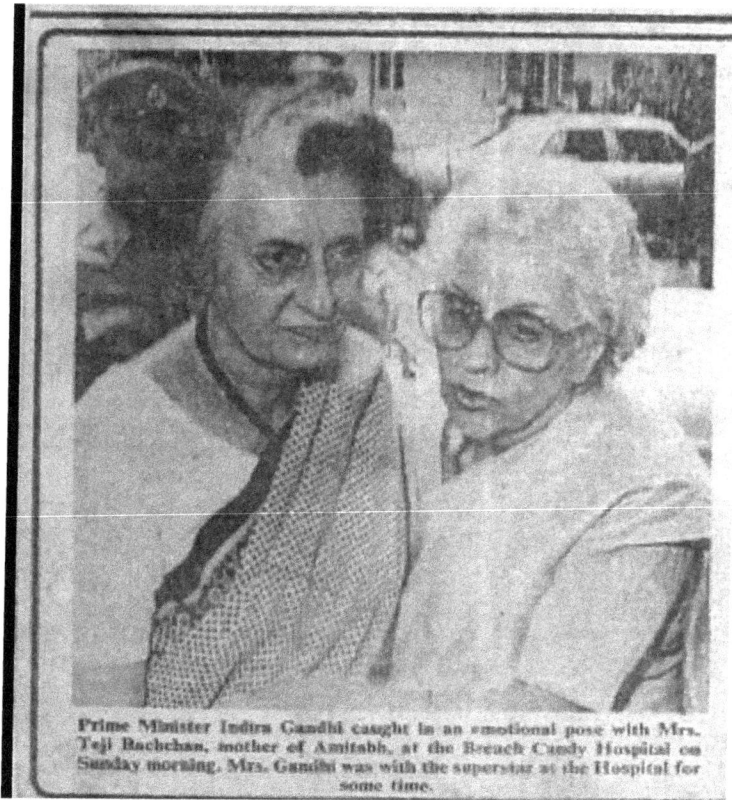

Prime Minister Indira Gandhi caught in an emotional pose with Mrs. Teji Bachchan, mother of Amitabh, at the Breach Candy Hospital on Sunday morning. Mrs. Gandhi was with the superstar at the Hospital for some time.

Monday, 9th August 1982, Day Sixteen

Article # 15. Indira visits ailing Amitabh

This was not an official visit by the Prime Minister of India for a popular Bollywood star who was fighting a battle for his life. The association and friendship between the Bachchan and Gandhi families went back decades. It all began when Sarojini Naidu (a prominent freedom fighter and a noted poet) introduced Harivansh Rai Bachchan and his wife Teji Bachchan to Nehru and a young Indira Gandhi.

Indira's father Jawaharlal Nehru, India's first Prime Minister, was very impressed with Amitabh's father, Mr. Harivansh Rai Bachchan, the poet. He called Mr. Bachchan to Delhi from Allahabad and posted him as an Officer on Special Duty in the Ministry of External Affairs in 1955.

Harivansh Rai Bachchan was a Ph.D. from Cambridge University, UK, where he did his doctoral research on poet W.B Yeats. After he returned to India, he took up a job teaching English Literature at Allahabad University.

In fact, it's been mentioned in a few articles that Indira Gandhi remembered her father Jawaharlal Nehru introducing Harivansh Rai to friends by saying, 'this is a poet' and pointing to Teji, he would add: 'and this is his poem!'

Teji Bachchan had earned fame as a tireless social activist and was known to be a close confidante and friend of Prime Minister Indira Gandhi.

Indira visits ailing Amitabh

By A Staff Reporter

Ailing Superstar Amitabh Bachchan acknowledged the visit of Prime Minister Indira Gandhi to the hospital by folding his hands in a "namaste" from the sick bed, on Sunday morning.

The Prime Minister, along with her daughter-in-law Sonia Gandhi, had flown to Bombay specifically to call on Amitabh Bachchan, who is fighting a life-and-death battle at the Breach Candy Hospital.

Amitabh also wrote a "thank you" note to the Prime Minister for her visit. As soon as she arrived at the hospital, Mrs. Gandhi was received at the foyer by the matinee idol's mother, Mrs. Teji Bachchan. They hugged each other before television cameras and waiting photographers. Mrs. Gandhi was then taken to the intensive care unit, where Amitabh is recovering.

After spending over 45 minutes at the hospital, meeting Amitabh's parents and relatives and going round it, Mrs. Gandhi drove straight to Raj Bhavan.

"Ask the doctors," she told waiting newsmen at the hospital, when asked about Amitabh's health. Mrs. Gandhi, along with Mrs. Sonia Gandhi, were in the ICU for about 15 minutes, according to the hospital's Medical Director, Jal Dubbash.

Amitabh could not talk to her as a tube had been inserted in his throat to help in his breathing. However, he was sitting on the bed with a backrest and was cheerful, according to Mr. Dubbash.

Later, Mrs. Gandhi spent another 15 minutes with Amitabh's parents and other family members, including his wife Jaya Bhaduri. The Prime Minister then visited the Godrej memorial ward at the Hospital.

A large crowd had gathered outside the hospital gates at Warden Road and all the surrounding sky-scrapers were filled with people, some with binoculars, craning their necks to watch the Prime Minister's visit to the Hospital.

After she had left for Raj Bhavan, the crowd tried to get into the hospital, but was not let in. As other film stars also started coming, the fans began to crowd around them, and the police had to drive them away.

The traffic on Warden Road was blocked for some time. There was heavy police bundobust around the Hospital and no one was allowed to enter inside. Only the Prime Minister's party and Chief Minister Babasaheb Bhosale were allowed inside.

Mr. Bhosale also flew in from the capital, along with the Prime Minister, in a special Indian Air Force aircraft. However, he came to the hospital about 15 minutes after the Prime Minister.

The hospital authorities said late at night on Sunday that there was a "little" improvement in Amitabh's health.

At the Santa Cruz airport, Mrs. Gandhi refused to accept garlands from some Congress (I) workers and the Mayor, remarking that it was not an occasion for flowers.

Mayor Prabhakar Pai later appealed to her to initiate measures to end the nearly seven-month-old textile strike in Bombay. The BJP Mayor handed over a memorandum to her.

However, leaving Raj Bhavan in the afternoon, after having lunch with the Governor, and Mrs. Teji Bachchan, Mrs. Gandhi told reporters that she was not aware of the latest position on the textile front, but would look into the matter.

She did not meet any political leaders at Raj Bhavan, according to sources.

After her four-hour visit to the city she left for Delhi and was seen off at the airport by the Governor and his wife, the Chief Minister and his Cabinet colleagues. Mrs. Teji Bachchan also accompanied her to the airport. (*Medical report:page 3*)

Monday, 9th August 1982, Day Sixteen

Article # 15. Indira visits ailing Amitabh (as transcribed from the article)

Ailing superstar Amitabh Bachchan acknowledged the visit of Prime Minister Indira Gandhi to the hospital by folding his hands in a "Namaste" from the sick bed, on Sunday morning. The Prime Minister, along with her daughter-in-law Sonia Gandhi, had flown to Bombay specifically to call on Amitabh Bachchan, who is fighting a life and death battle at the Breach Candy Hospital.

Amitabh also wrote a "thank you" note to the Prime Minister for her visit. As soon as she arrived at the hospital, Mrs. Gandhi was received at the foyer by the matinee idol's mother Mrs. Teji Bachchan. They hugged each other before television waiting photographers. Mrs. Gandhi was then taken to the Intensive Care Unit, where Amitabh is recovering.

After spending 45 minutes at the hospital, meeting Amitabh's parents and relatives and going around it, Mrs. Gandhi drove straight to Raj Bhavan.

"Ask the doctors", she told waiting newsmen at the hospital, when asked about Amitabh's health. Mrs. Gandhi, along with Mrs. Sonia Gandhi, were in the ICU for about 15 minutes, according to the hospital's Medical Director Jal Dubhash.

Amitabh could not talk to her as a tube had been inserted in his throat to help in his breathing. However, he was sitting on the bed with a backrest and was cheerful, according to Mr. Dubhash.

Later, Mrs. Gandhi spent another 15 minutes with Amitabh's parents and other family members, including his wife Jaya Bachchan. The Prime Minister then visited the Godrej memorial ward at the hospital.

A large crowd had gathered outside the hospital gates at Warden Road and all the surrounding sky-scrapers were filled with people, some with binoculars, craning their necks to watch the Prime Minister's visit to the Hospital.

After she had left for Raj Bhavan, the crowd tried to get into the hospital, but was not let in. As other film stars also started coming, the fans began to crowd around them, and police had to drive them away.

The traffic on Warden Road was blocked for some time. There was heavy police 'bandobust' around the Hospital and no one was allowed to enter inside. Only the Prime Minister's party and Chief minister Babasaheb Bhosale were allowed inside.

Mr. Bhosale also flew in from the capital, along with the Prime Minister, in a special Indian Air Force aircraft. However, he came to the hospital about 15 minutes after the Prime Minister.

The hospital authorities said late at night on Sunday that there was a "little" improvement in Amitabh's health.

At the Santa Cruz airport, Mrs. Gandhi refused to accept garlands from some Congress (I) workers and the Mayor, remarking that it was not an occasion for flowers.

Mayor Prabhakar Pai later appealed to her to initiate measures to ban the nearly seven-month-old textile strike in Bombay. The BJP Mayor handed over a memorandum to her.

However, leaving Raj Bhavan in the afternoon, after having lunch with Governor, and Mrs. Teji Bachchan, Mrs. Gandhi told reporters that she was not aware of the latest position on the textile front, but would look into the matter.

She did not meet any political leaders at Raj Bhavan, according to sources.

After her four-hour visit to the city she left for Delhi and was seen off at the airport by the Governor and his wife, the Chief Minister and his Cabinet colleagues, Mrs. Teji Bachchan also accompanied her to the airport.

Monday, 9th August 1982, Day Sixteen

Article # 16. Amitabh still critical

Film star Amitabh Bachchan is still "critical" doctors attending on him say. Amitabh's circulatory, respiratory and renal systems, though under considerable stress, had been kept in a stable condition.

The star still has sepsis in his abdominal cavity which is being "Adequately looked after", a medical bulletin issued on Sunday evening said.

The hospital authorities said that the pus formation in the actor's intestines continued resulting in infection and several other problems. The pus was being drained out through tubes every day.

Thousands of devotees of the Siddhi Vinayak Temple at Prabhadevi offered prayers on Sunday for the improvement in the health of Amitabh.

There were instances of film industry related events being cancelled as there was an atmosphere of sadness within the Bombay Film Industry:

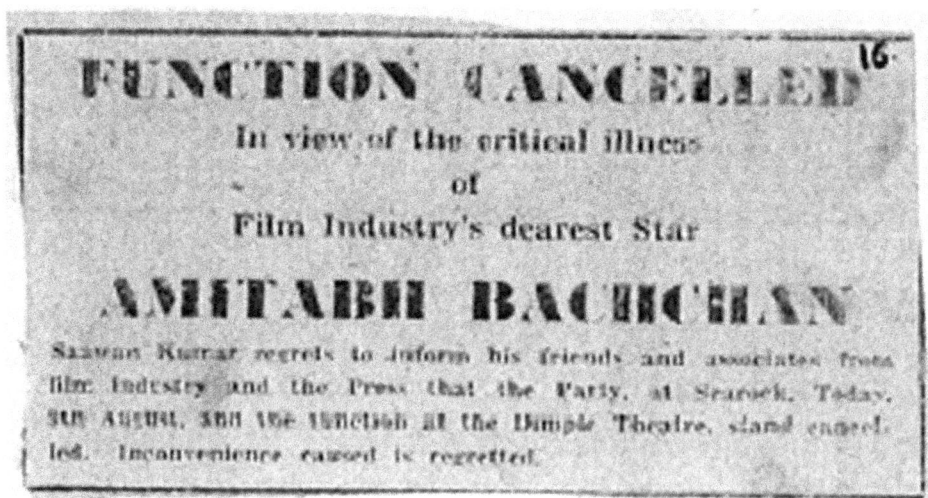

FUNCTION CANCELLED 16.
In view of the critical illness
of
Film Industry's dearest Star
AMITABH BACHCHAN
Saawan Kumar regrets to inform his friends and associates from film Industry and the Press that the Party, at Searock, Today, 8th August, and the function at the Dimple Theatre, stand cancelled. Inconvenience caused is regretted.

Amitabh still critical

By A Staff Reporter

Film star Amitabh Bachchan is still "critical", doctors attending on him say.

The 40-year-old Amitabh, who is undergoing treatment at Breach Candy hospital in Bombay for an intestinal injury suffered during a film shooting at Bangalore, still has sepsis in his abdomenal cavity which is being "Adequately looked after", a medical bulletin, issued on Sunday evening, said.

The actor's circulatory, respiratory and renal system, though under considerable stress, had been kept in a stable condition, the bulletin said.

The hospital authorities said that the pus formation in the actor's intestines continued resulting in infection and several other problems. The pus was being drained out through tubes every day, they explained.

Thousands of devotees of the Siddhi Vinayak at Prabhadevi offered prayers on Sunday for improvement in the health of Amitabh.

Tuesday, 10th August 1982 to Friday 13th August 1982, Day Seventeen to Day Twenty

Article # 17 to Article # 20 – Amitabh still serious, Amitabh better, Amitabh better, Amitabh improving

Amitabh's condition was still being described as "serious", but he did not require any respiratory support during the day.

The nurses who attended him reported (which usually means, the news is more accurate than any hospital bulletins) that Amitabh had shown every sign of recovery after the second operation. There were also reports that he would be flown to London for further analysis, where Amitabh's younger brother Ajitabh lived at that time.

It seemed like the prayers of his fans and well-wishers were taking effect. The next day was a much better day for Amitabh as he was weaned off his ventilator support. The Doctors attending on him did not think it necessary to call in 'Foreign specialists' though his medical reports were flown to London for further analysis. Amitabh's in-laws and several film personalities visited him at the hospital. His fans continued to surround the hospital, praying for Amitabh's speedy recovery.

It was good news as the week progressed and Amitabh continued to recover well. His health, as described by the hospital authorities, was 'satisfactory' and his cardiovascular, respiratory and renal systems were 'well maintained', though he was still in the intensive care unit. Amitabh looked 'more cheerful' during the day but was still on oral feeds. The outlook seemed promising and each day continued to look better than the previous day.

Several film stars visited Amitabh in hospital, among them were Shashi Kapoor, Ramesh Deo, Jalal Agha and Imtiaz Khan. Star-gazers and fans continued to swarm around the hospital and prayer meetings were held for his speedy recovery.

Amitabh Bachchan later revealed how this accident changed his life completely. It made such an impact on his health that the megastar still faces its aftermath to this day. 200 people donated 60 bottles of blood, but unfortunately, one of the donors was infected with the Hepatitis B virus. Amitabh recovered from the accident only to discover that the virus had resulted in liver cirrhosis.

Amitabh still serious 17

By A Staff Reporter

Film actor Amitabh Bachchan's condition continues to be "serious" but he does not need respiratory support during the day, a medical bulletin issued by the Breach Candy Hospital said on Monday evening.

Amitabh's cardio-vascular, respiratory and renal functions were "stable", the bulletin said.

Some nurses attending on him say that Amitabh has been showing every sign of recovering after the second operation last week.

Sources close to the actor said that Amitabh's medical reports would be flown to London tonight for further detailed analysis.

Amitabh 'better' 18

By A Staff Reporter

Amitabh Bachchan is now "better" and was put on oral feeds today, says a medical bulletin issued by the Breach Candy Hospital in the evening.

Amitabh was being "weaned" off ventilatory support, the bulletin says.

His medical reports were flown to London last night for pus and blood culture analysis. Howeve, one of the doctors attending on him said there was no need to call in a foreign specialist.

Amitabh's father-in-law Taroon Bhaduri, who is a journalist, and mother-in-law flew in from Lucknow to see him.

Several film personalities, including Shashi Kapoor, Ramesh Deo, Jalal Agha and Imtiaz Khan, called at the hospital to enquire about Amitabh's health.

Star-gazers continued to swarm around the hospital and some of them prayed Amitabh's speedy recovery.

Amitabh better 19

By A Staff Reporter

The condition of film star Amitabh Bachchan, undergoing treatment for abdominal injury at the Breach Candy Hospital, was described by the authorities as "satisfactory" on Wednesday evening.

Less pus was found in the tubes inserted in his abdominal cavity and the blood platelet count also remained steady, the Hospital sources said.

His cardio-vascular, respiratory and renal systems "are well maintained," the bulletin said adding that he was still under constant intensive care.

Amitabh looked "more cheerful" during the day. Though yet not out of danger, the film star continued to take an oral feed and if he continues to spend peaceful nights, then he might be given solid food.

Amitabh improving 20

By A Staff Reporter

Super Star Amitabh is improving. He is becoming more and more "conscious", one of the doctors attending on him at the Breach Candy Hospital in Bombay said on Thursday.

Amitabh would soon be given solid food, the doctor said.

The gastro-intestinal bleeding for which Amitabh was given blood transfusion on Wednesday should not cause any anxiety as it normally happened due to the anti-effect of life-saving drugs, the doctor pointed out.

Giants International held a prayer meeting on Thursday for the speedy recovery of Amitabh.

Saturday, 14th August 1982, Day Twenty-One

Article #21, Amitabh's condition worsens

Another setback. This time, the doctors found a "stress ulcer" in his stomach. His gastrointestinal bleeding had returned. The hospital issued a medical bulletin that described Amitabh as "seriously ill".

However, the doctors were positive and satisfied with the antibiotics given for the infection when he was first admitted. They had worked well and had removed the infection that had spread alarmingly through this body.

Amitabh still had the tracheotomy tube to help him breathe easily.

Sunday, 15th August 1982, Day Twenty-Two

Article # 22 and Article # 23, Amitabh's condition unchanged, Amitabh still serious

Today was 15th August! While India as a country was celebrating its 35th year of Independence, within the country Indians were very sad and in no mood for celebrations. The tragedy that had befallen one man had affected an entire nation. Their hero, their idol, their favorite star was still critical, fighting for his life, each day bringing on a new battle.

The further complications of a stress ulcer and recurrence of gastrointestinal bleeding caused considerable anxiety to all. This development put Amitabh back on the 'seriously ill' list.

Until Saturday, there were references to tubes attached to drain the infection out, but all references to these tubes were omitted from Sunday.

The situation remained unchanged from the setback suffered on previous day and Doctors were monitoring the stress ulcer very closely. They thought that it had potential to further complicate matters. Amitabh was under constant vigil after the turn of events from the previous day.

Amitabh's condition worsens 21

By A Staff Reporter

Film star Amitabh Bachchan suffered a setback on Friday with the doctors finding a "stress ulcer" in his stomach and his gastro-intestinal bleeding recurring.

A medical bulletin issued by the Breach Candy Hospital in Bombay on Friday evening said Amitabh continued to be "seriously ill" and under constant intensive medical care.

On Thursday the doctors attending on Amitabh had said that he was improving. On Friday morning also they said Amitabh was on "the road to recovery". However, an indoscopy during the day revealed the ulcer.

The buletin said: "the bleeding point was burnt in the hope that the bleeding does not recur." Amitabh's abdominal drain continued to discharge purulent material.

In the morning, a doctor had said "the most satisfactory thing about Amitabh's condition was that the medicine injected in him has successfully removed the infection which had spread alarmingly when he was admitted to the Hospital.

The tracheotomy tube, which helps Amitabh breath easily, would not, however, be removed unless the team of doctors felt he was out of danger.

Amitabh's condition unchanged 22

By A Staff Reprorter

The condition of Amitabh Bachchan was reported to be "unchanged" in a Breach Candy Hospital medical bulletin on Saturday, following a setback on Friday.

The single-sentence bulletin said that his condition remained unchanged. However, another hospital spokesman said that Amitabh was "improving." The hospital did not elaborate further on his condition.

According to hospital sources the doctors attending on the super-star had kept a constant vigil on him on Saturday, following a sudden turn for the worse the previous day.

They had found a "stress ulcer" in his stomach during endoscopic exmination, which could further complicate matters.

Amitabh[23] still serious

By A Staff Reporter

The detection of a stress ulcer and the recurrence of gastro-intestinal bleeding caused doctors attending on film star Amitabh Bachchan at Breach Candy Hospital considerable anxiety on Saturday.

Late in the evening, the bulletin stated that his condition "remained unchanged" and that he was back on the "seriously ill list".

Till Saturday the daily bulletin contained references to the tubes draining infection from his abdomen, but suddenly all reference to this was omitted.

Amitabh Bachchan suffered an intestinal injury while shooting a fight sequence for the film "Coolie" in Bangalore more than two weeks ago.

Sunday, 15th August 1982, Day Twenty-Two

Article # 24. Amitabh sets gossip mills buzzing (as transcribed from the article)

Matinee idol Amitabh Bachchan's grim fight for survival has set the gossip mill buzzing, revealing in the process the fascinating aspect of human nature, namely rumor mongering.

"It was no accident," goes one version, "Stuntman Puneet Issar, a karate black belt, did it deliberately with a deadly chop." Those who claim they were a witness in the accident and there are many such, as a recent visit to Bangalore revealed, dismissing the accident theory as hogwash.

"The report that the superstar fell heavily on the edge of the table is plain unadulterated bull," thereafter adding "It almost seemed as though the man was paid to do it". Yet another theory has it that a bullet was removed from Bachchan's stomach.

Theories as to the "sinister and behind the dastardly attempt' vary from possessive actresses to insidious political forces who are apprehensive that Bachchan's much-publicized intention to permanently wipe out the grease paint in favor of a career in politics may deal a mortal blow to their own political ambitions.

Then there are those who claimed they overheard Dr. Bhat reportedly on a visit to Bangalore's St. Philomena Hospital on some other work, exclaim, "You're giving me a dead man" on seeing Bachchan's condition. They insist that the star was permitted to return to the West End Hotel and operated on only after three days. And some, claiming to be in the know, assert that the renowned surgeon, having performed the surgery, left the comparatively unimportant work of tying the sutures to junior surgeons. And if these know-alls are to be believed, it is these very sutures which have been creating all the 'mischief' in the superstar's abdomen.

Of the fact that Bombay punters ever willing to have a flutter, bet heavily at Mahalaxmi last Sunday on whether or not the film star would survive, there is no doubt. But one is inclined to take with a large pinch of salt the gloomy prognostications of some soothsayers like Jammu Maharaj who claims he had warned Bachchan about his health in the latter half of July, going to the extent of saying that he would be seriously ill and that he would turn the corner on August 9.

Also the many revelations of 'friends' and 'witnesses' that actress 'X' managed to sneak into the Breach Candy Hospital's Intensive Care Unit or that ".." was turned out by suspicious wife Jaya Bhaduri. On and on in this absurd vein, the rumor mill grinds at society ladies coffee sessions as much as in the Chai shops.

Hundreds throng the hospital's entrance at Bhulabhai Desai Road and thousands pray for his recovery. Such is the 'Naseeb' of this 'Muqaddar ka Sikander' and to hell with the more important 'Roti, Kapada, Makaan' aspects of a humdrum existence.

Through all of this difficult period, Amitabh's wife Jaya kept her calm, presence of mind and one overriding statement, 'Doctor, please do whatever is essential. He is more important to us than anything else.' Jaya Bachchan stayed in the hospital all day, every day, taking notes about his condition, going through his reports, being the pillar of strength for her children and family. Despite the intense pressure and tension, she did not forget the small things, like sending flowers to Dr. Shah, when he finally went home after two long nights at the hospital, to express her gratitude.

SUNDAY MID-DAY, AUGUST 15, 1982

Amitabh sets gossip mill buzzing

MATINEE idol Amitabh Bachchan's grim fight for survival has set the gossip mill buzzing, revealing in the process a fascinating aspect of human nature, namely rumour-mongering.

"It was no accident," goes one version, "stuntman Puneet Issar, a karate black belt, did it deliberately with a deadly chop."

Those who claim they were witness to the incident—and there are many such as a recent visit to Bangalore revealed dismiss the accident theory as hogwash. "The report that the superstar fell heavily on the edge of the table is plain, unadulterated bull," they aver, adding "It almost seemed as though the man was paid to do it". Yet another theory has it that a bullet was removed from Bachchan's stomach.

Theories as to the 'sinister hand' behind the 'dastardly attempt' vary from possessive actresses to insidious political forces who are apprehensive that Bachchan's much-publicised intention to permanently wipe off the greasepaint in favour of a career in politics may deal a mortal blow to their own political ambitions.

Then there are those who claim they overheard Dr. Bhatt, reportedly on a visit to Bangalore's St. Philomena Hospital on some other work, exclaim, "You're giving me a dead man", on seeing Bachchan's condition. They insist that the star was permitted to return to the West End Hotel and operated on only after three days.

And some, claiming to be in the know, assert that the renowned surgeon, having performed the surgery, left the comparatively unimportant work of tying the sutures to junior surgeons. And if these know-alls are to be believed, it is these very sutures which have been creating all the 'mischief' in the superstar's abdomen.

Of the fact that Bombay punters, ever willing to have a flutter, bet heavily at Mahalaxmi last Sunday on whether or not the film star would survive, there is no doubt. But one is inclined to take with a large pinch of salt the gloomy prognostications of soothsayers like Jammu Maharaj who claims he had warned Bachchan about his health in the latter half of July, going to the extent of saying that he would be seriously ill and that he would turn the corner on August 9. Also the many revelations of 'friends' and 'witnesses' that actress 'X' managed to sneak into the Breach Candy Hospital's intensive care unit or that 'x' was turned out by suspicious wife Jaya Bhaduri.

On and on in this absurd vein the rumour-mill grinds at society ladies' coffee sessions as much as is the chai shops. Hundreds throng the hospital's entrance at Bhulabhai Desai Road every day. Giantspray for his recovery. Such is the 'nasoo' of this 'muqaddar ka sikandar' and to hell with the more important 'roti kapda, makaan' aspects of a humdrum existence.

Monday, 16th August 1982, Day Twenty-Three

Article # 26. Amitabh still serious

The news bulletin reported today that Amitabh Bachchan showed signs of improvement, though his condition still remained serious.

A doctor attending him said the bleeding in his intestines had recurred two days back and caused anxiety. This had been considerably controlled following an emergency 'cauterization' of his stress ulcer by two British gastroenterologists, who had flown in specially to examine him.

Other parameters were stable but his lungs were not free from complications and he remained in intensive care.

The visiting British doctors advised that the actor be flown to London, if his condition did not show clear improvement within the next day or two. But Amitabh's family were very happy with how the doctors at Breach Candy hospital were looking after him and they had full trust in their abilities.

Amitabh was once asked if he was confronted with the idea of his own mortality as stars often believe that they are immortal, he said, "When I did come out of hospital, I realized when I heard the stories and read the news, there was an unbelievable feeling of gratitude and even gratitude is sounding so less. I felt that this is a great burden that I will carry."

Amitabh still 28 serious

By A Staff Reporter

Matinee idol Amitabh Bachchan, who is convalescing at Breach Candy Hospital in Bombay, "showed signs of improvement", though "his condition still remained serious" according to a medical bulletin released by the hospital on Sunday evening.

Amitabh is undergoing treatment for intestinal injury.

A doctor attending on him said the bleeding in his intestines, which had recurred two days back and caused anxiety, had been considerably controlled following an emergency "cauterisation" of his "stress ulcer" by two British Gastroenterologists, who have flown specially to examine him.

According to the bulletin, his wounds were cleaner with "less discharge". But fluctuations in his condition were still anticipated. He was, therefore, still under intensive care.

The blood circulation of the cine star was reported to be stable and his kidney worked well.

However, his lungs were not free from complications, the hospital bulletin added.

Amitabh continued to be fed intravenously and orally.

Maharashtra Chief Minister Babasaheb Bhosale called on at Breach Candy Hospital to inquire about Amitabh Bachchan's condition.

Meanwhile, according to unofficial sources, the visiting British doctors have advised that the actor be flown to London, if condition does not show definite improvement within a day or two.

Tuesday, 17th August 1982 to Friday, 20th August 1982, Day Twenty-Four to Day Twenty-Seven

Article # 27 to Article # 30 - Amitabh better, Amitabh's condition unchanged, Amitabh, Amitabh better

Amitabh's condition improved considerably from Sunday, though he remained in intensive care and was 'not out of danger'. His vital parameters were stable and the gastrointestinal wound appeared to be healing.

The two London-based specialists, Dr. M Williams and Dr. J Peter, who had flown in to examine the actor, returned to London.

Amitabh's wound was reported to be better and his gastrointestinal bleeding appeared to be gone for good. The medical bulletin, however, reported that his condition remained unchanged. He was still being fed intravenously.

His fans continued to throng the hospital throughout the day, waiting for news of his health. There were reports from the hospital stating the star developed lung problems and his condition remained serious. However, the bulletin also reported "the general condition of Amitabh was better" and there was considerable improvement.

As the week progressed, it was reported that Amitabh was improving and feeling better. His lung complications had shown improvement and he was gradually being weaned off the intravenous feed and had some solid food.

Amitabh better

By A Staff Reporter 27

The condition of actor Amitabh Bachchan improved considerably on Monday though he continues to be "not out of danger", according to a medical bulletin of Breach Candy Hospital where he is undergoing treatment for intestinal injury.

The actor had shown more signs of improvement but was still in the intensive care unit of the hospital it added.

Amitabh's gastro-intestinal wound appeared to be better on Monday. His circulation was stable and the kidneys were functioning well.

Meanwhile, the two London-based specialists, Dr. M. Williams and Dr. J. Peter, who examined the actor, have left for London after the examination, according to family sources.

Amitabh's condition unchanged

28

By A Staff Reporter

The condition of Amitabh Bachchan remained unchanged on Tuesday, according to a medical bulletin issued by the Breach Candy Hospital in the evening.

His wound was reported to be better than what it was four to five days back, but it still continued to discharge pus. "Fortunately there has been no recurrence of gastro-intestinal bleeding since Monday afternoon," the bulletin added.

The superstar continued to be nourished orally and was fed intravenously. His fans continued to throng the hospital throughout the day, anxiously awaiting to get some news.

Amitabh

29

By A Staff Reporter

Amitabh Bachchan has developed lung problems and his condition remained serious, a bulletin issued on Wednesday night by the Breach Candy Hospital said.

His lung problem was directly related to his abdominal sepsus. However the general condition of the actor was "better". There was considerable improvement as compared to Tuesday, the bulletin stated.

Amitabh better

30

By A Staff Reporter

The condition of filmstar Amitabh Bachchan has been described as "better" by the Breach Candy Hospital, where he is convalescing for his abdominal injury.

Amitabh's pulmonary complication has also showed improvement and he was put on adequately nourishing diet, requiring very little fluid to be given intravenously, a medical bulletin of the hospital stated.

Saturday, 21st August 1982 and Sunday, 22nd August 1982, Day Twenty-Eight and Day Twenty-Nine

Article # 31 to Article # 33 - Amitabh has fever, Amitabh out of danger, Amitabh given blood transfusion

Though Amitabh developed a fever, he had considerably improved from the other complications. His windpipe tube was removed and he could breathe without its aid. The doctors also mentioned that the star may be shifted out of the intensive care unit in two weeks.

Amitabh suffered from recurrent bleeding and had to be given a blood transfusion. However, his general condition had improved and he was improving satisfactorily. They also mentioned that he might be shifted from the intensive care unit soon.

Some of the blood from an unknown donor was infected with the Australian antigen Hepatitis. This particular infection had the quality of getting active inside the system after lying dormant for a couple of months. "It was also an unknown hepatitis virus in 1982 and there were, perhaps due to the urgency of the matter, no known immediate tests to ascertain its existence before it was administered. So, it went into my system, festered and attacked my liver and as a result, I developed cirrhosis of the liver - a condition that is normally associated with that of an alcoholic. So here I was, a non-alcoholic, a teetotaller, with an ailment that I imbibed through a blood transfusion from a donor," said Amitabh Bachchan."

Amitabh has fever [31]

By A Staff Reporter

Film star Amitabh Bachchan's condition remained "essentially unchanged" on Friday, according to a hurriedly read Medical Bulletin on the telephone by the Breach Candy Hospital authorities.

Mr. Bachchan is running fever due to his abdominal problem.

However, according to unconfirmed reports Mr. Bachchan had showed considerable signs of improvement as the tube inserted in his windpipe was removed and he could breath without its aid. He also took solid diet on Friday.

Amitabh out of danger [33]

BOMBAY, Aug. 21:
Matinee idol Amitabh Bachchan is "out of danger" and his condition is improving satisfactorily, according to a doctor attending on him at the Breach Candy Hospital here.

Amitabh's gastro-intestinal bleeding has now been completely controlled. The pus discharge from his abdominal wound was "much less", the doctors said.

Except that he still had fever, all other systems were functioning normally. The doctors added that the actor might be shifted from the intensive care unit after two weeks. UNI

Amitabh given [32] blood transfusion

By A Staff Reporter

Filmstar Amitabh Bachchan suffered from recurrent gastro-intestinal bleeding and had to be given blood transfusion, stated a medical bulletin issued by the Breach Candy Hospital on Saturday.

However his general condition improved.

Meanwhile, according to unconfirmed reports, Mr. Bachchan is "out of danger" and his condition is improving satisfactorily." He might be shifted from the intensive care unit soon.

The actor's intestines had been ruptured during the shooting of a fight sequence of Hindi film Coolie in Bangalore on July 26. He was admitted to the Breach Candy Hospital on July 31.

Monday, 23rd August 1982, Day Thirty

Article # 34. Amitabh under strict vigil

The continuous build-up of pressure and concern over Amitabh's recovery process from the previous weeks eased up a little. There was mention of moving Amitabh out of the intensive care unit bringing a feeling of relief, but reports of finding a stress ulcer caused anxiety at the same time.

"Even as things brightened up a little on the Amitabh Bachchan front at the Breach Candy Hospital amid a general feeling of relief, Amitabh suffered a setback and there was cause for anxiety again".

An endoscopy performed on the superstar, previously on August 13, showed a stress ulcer which put the team of doctors attending him on the alert. They kept a strict vigil on him. At the time of going to press, the health bulletin said his condition remained unchanged, which was a vague explanation to avoid complications. Sources close to his family, however, maintained that "he is improving and if all went well and God willing, Amitabh would be out of the intensive care unit in fifteen days,"

Earlier too on August 14, the anxiety caused was intolerable when doctors and other authorities at the hospital were tight-lipped, "mainly because of embarrassing reports in a section of the press".

From Amitabh's son, Abhishek Bachchan's twitter feed (2017)

When I used to visit my father after his accident on the sets of "Coolie" in 1982, seeing him connected to many drips and machines, he used to tell me they were kites that he had got for me. I was 6 years old. My father was fighting for his life and all I thought about was "why isn't he allowing me to play with these kites??? The innocence of childhood I guess"

Amitabh under strict vigil

By ALI PETER JOHN

EVEN as things brightened up a little on the Amitabh Bachchan front at the Breach Candy Hospital and there was a general feeling of relief, Amitabh suffered a set back and there was cause for anxiety again. An endoscopy performed on the superstar on August 13 showed a stress ulcer which put the team of doctors attending on him on the alert. The vigil kept on him became very strict. At the time of going to press, the health bulletin issued said his condition remained unchanged which was a vague explanation to avoid complications. Sources close to his family, however, maintained that "he is improving and if all went well and God willing, Amitabh would be out of the intensive care unit in fifteen days." Anxiety was intolerable on August 14 when doctors and other authorities at the hospital were tight-lipped "mainly because of embarrassing reports in a section of the press".

Tuesday, 24th August 1982 to Friday, 27th August 1982, Day Thirty-One to Day Thirty-Four

Article # 35 to Article # 38 - Amitabh better, Amitabh recovering, Amitabh progressing, Amitabh improving

It was exactly a month from today, that Amitabh got hurt.

Everybody had come a long way. It was a month full of tension-filled days, night-long vigils, of prayers and hope overcoming despair. The doctors and their star patient were fighting life together not prepared to lose, ultimately battling death and winning!

This week was much better as Amitabh's condition showed further improvements and he was becoming more and more cheerful.

On Sunday, 22nd August, Amitabh walked for the first time since being admitted.

Amitabh spent a restful night, had his first proper meal on Monday and was feeling much better. Steady progress had been made towards recovery and his condition was satisfactory, said the hospital bulletin. However, the star was still in intensive care. In view of his remarkable progress, the hospital authorities discontinued the daily medical bulletin about his health.

The feeding tubes were removed, and the wound was healing well. It was reported that Amitabh had a nourishing breakfast in the morning, enjoying his porridge, eggs, milk, idli, and rice which was a very good sign. He also listened to music when he was awake. It was also the first day he had his walking exercise for which he needed no support.

Though Amitabh's condition was improving, he was still in intensive care.

Amitabh better 35
By A Staff Reporter

Film star Amitabh Bachchan's condition showed further improvement, Breach Candy hospital sources, said on Monday night.

He is becoming more and more cheerful, a doctor attending him, said.

"There was no gastro-intestinal bleeding now and the pus discharge from his abdominal was also very low," the doctor said.

Amitabh, on Sunday, walked for the first time since his admission to the hospital and was made to walk on Monday, too.

He was given nutritious diet for the first time on Monday.

Amitabh recovering 36
By A Staff Reporter

Film Star Amitabh Bachchan's condition is satisfactory and he is making steady progress towards recovery, according to a Breach Candy hospital source, on Tuesday.

However he is still in the intensive care unit of the hospital. In view of his remarkable progress, the hospital authorities have discontinued daily medical bulletin about his health.

Amitabh progressing 37
By A Staff Reporter

Film star Amitabh Bachchan spent a restful night on Tuesday and was feeling better on Wednesday morning, according to the Breach Candy hospital source, on Wednesday.

"He, had a nourishing breakfast this morning", it was stated.

UNI adds: A doctor attending on the actor told UNI today that the tube, which had been inserted for feeding, had been removed. His wound was "progressing well" and the pus discharge was also reducing steadily every day.

He enjoys his porridge, eggs, milk, idli and rice and listens to music when he is awake. He had his walking exercise today also, for which he needed no support, the doctor added.

Amitabh improving 38
By A Staff Reporter

Film star Amitabh Bachchan's condition is steadily improving, according to the Breach Candy hospital sources, on Thursday.

"However he is still in the intensive care unit", it was stated.

Monday, 30th August 1982 to Sunday, 5th September 1982, Day Thirty-Seven to Day Forty-Three

Article # 39 to Article # 44 - Amitabh breathes fresh air, Amitabh cheerful, Amitabh Progresses, Amitabh improves

This week started on a very positive note when Amitabh took in fresh air today for the first time since his hospitalization. He was taken for x-rays to another floor, where he was taken around the podium. The x-rays showed no further complications.

Amitabh is now 'bored at the hospital" and would not mind "some shooting" at the Breach Candy itself. This sentiment warmed the hearts of his family and friends as it showed Amitabh returning back to his usual self, showing his mock enthusiasm for work.

He was reported to be in good spirits, walked around and could even talk, with all his tubes now 'disconnected". The authorities indicated that the superstar would be out of the intensive care unit in about 10 to 12 days.

Amitabh's family said there were no plans to take him abroad for further treatment.

Rumors on Amitabh's health still doing the rounds.

From the time the press got to know of Amitabh Bachchan's hospitalization, it buzzed with stories, which were excessively gloomy. This was because the press lacked briefing. The Breach Candy hospital operators answered the phone with, "Please don't pester us". No one was pestering them—the press was only doing their job in public interest.

Then Amitabh gave the first definitive interview to The Times of India. Apart from enjoying the morbid humor of his own situation, Amitabh said he thought he might not be able to face the camera ever again. Here 'might' was obviously the operative word, and what Amitabh said was the only honest thing he could possibly have said in the circumstances. Soon enough, his directors Prakash Mehra and Manmohan Desai were saying in their interviews that nothing was seriously wrong with Amitabh, all he needed was some rest and then he would be back on the sets.

Amitabh breathes fresh air

BOMBAY, Aug. 30 (UNI).
Hindi film star Amitabh Bachchan breathed fresh air today for the first time after his hospitalisation here for treatment of an intestinal injury he suffered during a shooting at Bangalore last month.

Sources at the Breach Candy Hospital in south Bombay tonight said Amitabh was brought down in a wheel chair from the intensive care unit for an x-ray. He was taken around the podium.

A doctor attending on Amitabh told UNI that the actor's condition was much better now. The x-ray photograph showed no further complications.

The discharge of pus from his wound was also less, he added.

Amitabh cheerful

By A Staff Reporter
Superstar Amitabh Bachchan is "bored at the hospital," and would not mind "some shooting" at the Breach Candy Hospital itself.

A cheerful Amitabh expressed his boredom a few day's back to another Hindi filmstar who called on him at the hospital. The visitor found Amitabh to be his usual self as indicated by his mock enthusiasm for work.

Film industry circles are extremely happy that the crisis has blown over. Amitabh walked around on Sunday and can even talk now, according to hospital and film sources.

It is also learnt that he will be out of the Intensive Care Unit in about 10 to 12 days. His family has no plans to take him abroad for treatment, said a source close to the family.

Amitabh progresses
43

BOMBAY, Sept. 2 (UNI).
Cine star Amitabh Bachchan, is improving, a doctor attending on him said tonight.

He had a 'little' cough due to post-operational complications in his lung, but he is 'perfectly all right', the doctor said.

Amitabh improves
44

By A Staff Reporter

Breach Candy Hospital sources reported improvement in the condition of filmstar Amitabh Bachchan on Sunday night.

Monday, 6th September 1982, Day Forty-Four

Article # 45. 'From gloom to jubilation... over Amitabh' (as transcribed from the article)

Filmstar Amitabh Bachchan, who has almost completely recovered from his problems, may still take at least three months to report back for work, according to sources in the film industry.

In spite of this, there is general jubilation at his industry particularly among the producers and directors who had made large investments with him in the cast.

Breach Candy Hospital, where the actor is since July 31, at last wears a look of jubilation with smiling crowds, in contrast to early about a fortnight back when the Hospital wore a pale of gloom.

The actor himself is said to look particularly cheerful, though considerably weak after the long struggle with death.

In another 10 days, he may be out of the Intensive Care Unit and may even be discharged from the hospital itself. More so because large crowds of his fans are creating problems for other patients of the hospital.

Amitabh has started entertaining some personal friends too besides the family members.

His greatest asset, his voice, is normal and he may start dubbing for two of his films, *Nastik* and *Mahan* within a month.

Jaya Bachchan, his wife who only a couple of days back was tense and anxious, is seen more relaxed now.

Amitabh himself has remarked about the uncompleted films. He is reported to be asking friends about the film *Coolie* during the shooting of which he received the injury.

From gloom to jubilation... over Amitabh

By A Staff Reporter

Filmstar Amitabh Bachchan, who has almost completely recovered now and has no post discharge problems, may still take at least three months to report back for work, according to sources in the film industry.

In spite of this, there is general jubilation at his recovery, particularly among the producers and directors who had made large investments with him in the cast.

Breach Candy Hospital, where the actor is convalescing since July 31 last wears a look of jubilation with smiling crowds, in contrast to only about a fortnight back when the Hospital wore a pale of gloom.

The actor himself is said to look particularly cheerful, though considerably weak, after the long struggle with death.

In another 10 days he may be out of the Intensive Care Unit and may even be discharged from the Hospital itself, more so because large crowds of his fans are creating problems for other patients of the hospital.

Amitabh has started entertaining some personal friends too besides the family members.

His greatest asset, his voice, is normal and he may start dubbing for two of his films, "Nastik" and "Maan" within a month.

Jaya Bachchan, his wife who only a couple of days back was tense and anxious, is seen more relaxed now.

Amitabh himself is concerned about the uncompleted films. He is reported to be asking friends about the film Coolie during the shooting of which he received the injury.

Tuesday, 7th September 1982, Day Forty-Five

Article # 46. Amitabh releases cassette

This was a much better day for Amitabh as he was able to now walk within the corridors without any assistance. He was also off the oral feeds, though still on a liquid diet. In fact, he also released his album recordings for his performance shows held earlier in the year in USA and West Indies. He mentioned, "It is indeed my pleasure to formally release the music cassette and the double album. I hope that all those who listened to the show captured on the live recording will enjoy them as much as I do."

From his hospital bed, Amitabh formally released this album titled: Live Tonite - Amitabh Bachchan Vol 1

The vinyl record and cassette were recordings of Amitabh's stage shows with music directors Kalyanji-Anandji, held in USA, Canada, and West Indies.

In fact, these music directors together with Amitabh were one of the first to start the trend of elaborate world tours of live in concert stage shows. Together they created history when they performed Bollywood songs to Calypso & Reggae style beats.

Amitabh releases cassette

By A Staff Reporter

Filmstar Amitabh Bachchan might remain in the intensive care unit, of the Breach Candy Hospital for another two weeks, a hospital source said on Tuesday night.

The doctors are likely to decide by the weekend about his discharge from the Hospital now that the intestinal injury he suffered during a shooting in Bangalore had dried. There is no deischarge of pus also.

Amitabh is now able to walk without any aid and is able to eat a few solids, though is food his predominantly liquid.

The actor on Tuesday released a cassette and a double album entitled "live tonite-Amitabh Bachchan" in the hospital itself. The album contains the recording of Amitabh's shows staged, along with the music directors Kalyanji-Anandji, in the US, Canada and West Indies.

He cut a ribbon to release the cassette and the record. A record was also presented to him.

In a signed note, the superstar said "it is indeed my pleasure to formally release the music cassette and the double album. I hope that all those who listened to the show captured on the live recording will enjoy them as much as I did."

Monday, 20th September 1982, Day Fifty-Eight

Article # 47. Amitabh to be discharged by week-end (as transcribed from the article)

Amitabh Bachchan is expected to leave the Breach Candy Hospital by the end of the week.

On September 24, he completes exactly three (sic) two months since hospitalization following a serious internal injury while shooting for the film *Coolie* in Bangalore. Hospital sources discounted reports published in a section of the press that he would be discharged on Tuesday or Wednesday.

Amitabh has made a remarkable recovery and is reported to be in good spirits. However, he is still in the Intensive Care Unit of the hospital. The superstar has been able to walk short distances on his own and then managed to climb a flight of stairs. His diet has been restored to normal. He is allowed to meet his relatives and friends although for short periods.

Amitabh has expressed his gratitude for the overwhelming affection and good wishes of his many fans and well-wishers. The actor continues to receive the messages, flowers and even small gifts from numerous admirers and well-wishers. Although there are rumors that he is going to convalesce abroad, indications are that he will continue to remain in Bombay for at least a month.

47

Amitabh to be discharged by week-end

By A Staff Reporter

Amitabh Bachchan is expected to leave the Breach Candy Hospital by the end of the week.

On September 24, he completes exactly three months since hospitalisation following a serious internal injury while shooting for the film "Coolie" in Bangalore.

Hospital sources discounted reports published in a section of the Press that he would be discharged on Tuesday or Wednesday.

Amitabh has made a remarkable recovery and is reported to be in good spirits. However, he is still in the intensive care unit of the hospital. The superstar has been able to walk short distances on his own and even managed to climb a flight of stairs. His diet has been restored to normal. He is allowed to meet his relatives and friends, although for short periods.

Amitabh has expressed his gratitude for the overwhelming affection and good wishes of his many fans and well-wishers. The actor continues to receive messages, flowers and even small gifts from numerous admirers and well-wishers.

Although there are rumours that he is going to convalesce abroad, indications are that he will continue to remain in Bombay for at least a month.

Wednesday, 22nd September 1982, Day Sixty

Article # 48. Amitabh's gesture to hospital

As a gesture of his gratitude and goodwill, the actor has in advance donated the first day's collections of his next film *Shakti* to the St. Philomena Hospital in Bangalore.

The Superstar's gesture comes in the wake of the controversy over the treatment given to him in Bangalore.

An emissary of the star travelled to Bangalore to convey this to the Hospital Superintendent. Amitabh and Jaya were keen on making this donation as they felt that the treatment at the Hospital paved the way for the film star's eventual recovery.

Amitabh Bachchan had donated generously towards the improvement of St. Philomena's hospital and now it is one of the most sought-after hospitals in Bangalore. Years later, Julie, the nurse who looked after him, was hospitalized and had no one to care for her after her husband died. The old age home, Humanitarian Hands, wrote a report on her. On reading the report, the superstar immediately sent a cheque of Rs. 2 lakh (Rs. 200,000) for her treatment and invited her to visit him.

Amitabh's gesture to hospital 48

BANGALORE, Sept. 22 (UNI).

As a gesture of his gratitude, and good will, Hindi matinee idol Amitabh Bachchan, now convalescing in Bombay, has in advance donated the first day's collections of his next film "Shakti" to the St. Philomena Hospital here.

Mr. Bachchan has made the gesture to the Hospital where he was first admitted on July 26 after he suffered a grievous intestinal injury during the shooting of the film "Coolie" here.

The super star's gesture comes in the wake of the controversy in a section of the press over the treatment given to him in Bangalore.

Superintendent of the St. Philomena Hospital Dr. C. D. Jacob told UNI that an emissary of Mr Bachchan personally came down from Bombay to convey to him that Mr. Bachchan and his actress-wife Jayabadhuri were keen on making the donation. They felt that the treatment at the Hospital paved the way for the film star's eventual recovery.

Friday, 24th September 1982, Day Sixty-Two

September 24, the day Amitabh Bachchan was discharged from the Intensive Care Unit of Breach Candy Hospital was a day of triumph and joy, not only for the Bachchans but also for countless people who prayed for his full recovery, and Amitabh, who is seen here surrounded by his cheering admirers, said he had no words to express his gratitude to his fans who had stood lovingly by his side while he fought desperately for life in the hospital. Picture shows Amitabh, looking as intense as ever, emerging from the I.C. Unit.

DAY OF JOY

September 24, the day Amitabh Bachchan was discharged from the Intensive Care Unit of Breach Candy Hospital was a day of triumph and joy not only for the Bachchans but also for countless people who prayed for his full recovery, and Amitabh, who is seen here surrounded by cheering admirers, said he had no words to express his gratitude to his fans who stood lovingly by his side while he fought desperately for life in the hospital. Picture shows Amitabh, looking as intense as ever, emerging from the I.C. Unit.

As expected, it was not easy for the actor to reach his car. He waved out to his fans, acknowledged their cheers and waded his way through a sea of humanity to reach the car, waiting to take him home. According to witnesses Amitabh was "visibly moved" by the affection of his fans. It was the first time in two months that the actor was coming out in the open.

As expected, it was not easy for the actor to reach his car. He waved out to his fans, acknowledged their cheers and waded his way through a sea of humanity to reach the car, waiting to take him home. According to witnesses Amitabh was "visibly moved" by the affection of his fans. It was the first time in two months that the actor was coming out in the open.
Photos by Saby Fernandez and V. Ramaswamy.

"If it had been anybody else, he would have succumbed," added Ramesh Sippy. "You don't know what a fighter Amitabh is. He just never gives up."

Taking Papa home

While two little fans of the actor wait patiently (left) to give him flowers as he comes out of the ICU, Amitabh's children, Abhishek and Shweta (right) are escorted inside the hospital premises by a family friend.

Taking papa home: While two little fans of the actor wait patiently (left) to give him flowers as he comes out of the ICU, Amitabh's children, Abhishek and Shweta (right) are escorted inside the hospital premises by a family friend.

"It is only his will-power that has pulled him through," said Yash Johar, who had rushed to Bangalore with spare doses of platelet-rich plasma and had stayed with the family through their most anxious moments.

Friday, 24th September 1982, Day Sixty-Two

Article # 51. Amitabh leaves hospital (as transcribed from the article)

"Two months of hospitalization and the terrible ordeal of fighting a battle for survival are over, I am going home today", reads a part of the Press release issued by Amitabh Bachchan who left the Breach Candy Hospital in Bombay on September 24 for his residence at Juhu.

The matinee idol, who had been admitted to the hospital on July 31 after he had sustained an intestinal rupture during the shooting of Manmohan Desai's *Coolie* in Bangalore, was discharged from the hospital at 11:30 a.m. "He has fully recovered from his illness and after a period of rest and convalescence should be able to resume in full swing his professional activities", says a medical bulletin released on the occasion.

The Breach Candy Hospital, which for the last two months had been the center of attraction for Amitabh's countless fans, was literally swarmed by a crowd of about three thousand people since morning. All were eagerly waiting to see their favorite superstar emerging victorious after he had fought with death battle for his life in the Intensive Care Unit in the second floor of the hospital. Their solemn faces lit up in smiles as Amitabh, clad in churidar-kurta with a shawl wrapped round his shoulder, appeared in the foyer accompanied by his wife Jaya, their children Abhishek and Shweta, Manmohan Desai, Prakash Mehra, and Yash Johar.

There was a stampede among the photographers to shoot the best photograph, the first since he had been admitted to the hospital.

The people, as soon as they spotted Amitabh, rushed forward breaking the cordon of the police and security men to see him from close quarters.

Amitabh stood amidst them for a while, waved at them, showed his clenched fist by raising his right hand as if to mean that the victory ultimately was his, that he was absolutely hale and hearty. However, the actor seemed to have lost a lot of weight. But for that, he looked fresh and relaxed. He had cut his hair short and his face was clean shaven as usual.

Amitabh leaves hospital

By JIVRAJ BURMAN

"TWO months of hospitalisation and the terrible ordeal of fighting a battle for survival are over. I am going home today," reads a part of the Press release issued by Amitabh Bachchan who left the Breach Candy Hospital in Bombay on September 24 for his residence at Juhu. The matinee idol, who had been admitted to the hospital on July 31 after he had sustained an intestinal rupture during the shooting of Manmohan Desai's "Coolie" in Bangalore, was dis-

(Continued on Page 10)

(Continued from Page 1)
charged from the hospital at 11.30 a.m. "He has fully recovered from his illness and after a period of rest and convalescence should be able to resume in full swing his professional activities," says a medical bulletin released on the occasion.

The Breach Candy Hospital, which for the last two months had been the centre of attraction for Amitabh's countless fans, was literally swarmed by a crowd of about three thousand people since morning. All were eagerly waiting to see their favourite super star emerging victorious after he had fought with death a battle for his life in the intensive care unit in the second floor of the hospital. Their solemn faces lit up in smiles as Amitabh, clad in churidar-kurta with a shawl wrapped round his shoulder, appeared in the foyer accompanied by his wife Jaya, their children Abhishek and Shweta, Manmohan Desai, Prakash Mehra and Yash Johar.

There was a stampede among the photographers to shoot the best photograph, the first since he had been admitted to the hospital. The people, as soon as they

---

"God is great, Amit is back"

The reigning superstar of India's Hollywood – Amitabh Bachchan was going back home today at the end of a two-month hospitalization and his 'terrible ordeal of fighting for survival'.

Dressed in a white kurta-pyjama and a shawl draped around him, Amitabh emerged out of the Breach Candy Hospital, looking pale but cheerful and raised his clenched fist in the air in a symbol of victory.

Reacting to the love, affection, wishes, and prayers of millions of people, Amitabh later released a statement to the press saying "I am overwhelmed. It is impossible for me to repay this debt. The least I can do is try and live up to your expectations."

AN EVENT

A white Ambassador car, MMU 7216, drove right up to the foyer. Amitabh clasped his hands to say "Namaste" and briskly got into the car followed by Jaya, the children, and Manmohan Desai. The car whirred past the crowd immediately. The Breach Candy Hospital suddenly looked deserted. The doctors, sisters, nurses and ward boys watched the car as it moved out of the hospital gate. Soon all the other cars of Amitabh's well-wishers who had come to congratulate him on his recovery drove past one by one. An event had just ended at Breach Candy Hospital which during the two months it lasted had seen many tears shed, many prayers and until at last it saw smiles all around. Outside the hospital there was a festoon in red lettering "God is great, Amit is back." *Amitabh's recovery can certainly be attributed to God's great benevolence.* Many a time during the past two months the condition of his health fluctuated, causing anxiety to the members of his family, well-wishers, fans, and even the doctors attending on him. The anxiety ran high at one time there was a steep fall in the platelet cells in his blood and he developed other complications like stress ulcer.

News of Amitabh's accident first appeared in Bombay newspaper on July 26 when he was operated upon at the St. Philomena's Hospital in Bangalore after he had sustained the injuries in his stomach during the shooting of *Coolie* on July 24. The frequent news, thereafter, of his fluctuating conditions of health shook the entire film industry in Bombay, where a few big budget films were in the process of being made with the super star in the lead.

His condition at times, plunged the entire nation in sorrow, from the common man to Prime Minister Mrs. Indira Gandhi. In every nook and corner of the country his fans held prayers for his speedy recovery. Some of them even offered their own life if that could save the life of Amitabh.

The untiring efforts of the doctors at St. Philomena and Breach Candy Hospitals, the faith of innumerable fans in God, the fervent prayers of his family members and his own will power brought Amitabh well on the road to recovery. And today September 24, after two months, "the superstar", "the phenomenon", could walk ramrod straight, could climb down the stairs all by himself from the second floor of the hospital which he had entered on a stretcher, weak and unconscious.

He had enacted in real life death-defying scene, as it were, as he had done a number of times on the screen. He lived up to his screen image of a "tough man".

"God is great, Amit is back"

spotted Amitabh, rushed forward breaking the cordon of the police and security men to see him from close quarters. Amitabh stood amidst them for a while, waved at them, showed his clenched fist by raising his right hand, as if to mean that the victory ultimately was his, that he was absolutely hale and hearty. However, the actor seemed to have lost a lot of weight. But for that he looked fresh and relaxed. He had cut his hair short and his face was clean shaven as usual.

AN EVENT

A white Ambassador car, MMU 7216, drove right up to the foyer. Amitabh clasped his hands to say "Namaste" and briskly got into the car followed by Jaya Bhaduri, the children and Manmohan Desai. The car whirred past the crowd immediately. The Breach Candy Hospital suddenly looked deserted. The doctors, sisters, nurses and ward boys watched the car as it moved out of the hospital gate. Soon all the other cars of Amitabh's well-wishers who had come to congratulate him on his recovery drove past one by one. An event had just ended at the Breach Candy Hospital which during the two months it lasted had seen many tears shed, many prayers said until at last it saw smiles all around.

Outside the hospital there was a festoon in red lettering, "God is great, Amit is back." Amitabh's recovery can certainly be attributed to God's great benevolence. Many a time during the past two months the condition of his health fluctuated, causing anxiety to the members of his family, well-wishers, fans, and even the doctors attending on him. The anxiety ran high at one time there was a steep fall in the platelet cells in his blood and he developed other complications like stress ulcer.

News of Amitabh's accident first appeared in Bombay newspapers on July 26 when he was operated upon at the St. Philomena's Hospital in Bangalore after he had sustained the injuries in his stomach during the shooting of "Coolie" on July 24. The frequent news, thereafter, of his fluctuating conditions of health shook the entire film industry in Bombay where a few big budget films were in the process of being made with the super star in the lead. His condition at ti... plunged the entire nation in ... row, from the common man ... Prime Minister Mrs. Indira Ga... hi. In every nook and corner of ... country his fans held prayers ... his speedy recovery. Some ... them even offered their own li... if that could save the life ... Amitabh.

The untiring efforts of the d... tors at St. Philomena's and Brea... Candy Hospitals, the faith of ... innumerable fans in God, the ... lent prayers of his family mem... ers and his own will pow... brought Amitabh well on the ro... to recovery. And today, Se... tember 24, after two months, t... super star, "The phenomenon" ... could walk ramrod straight, co... climb down the stairs all ... himself from the second floor ... the hospital which he had ente... on a stretcher, weak and unc... scious.

He had enacted in real life ... death-defying scene, as it we... as he had done a number ... times on the screen. He lived ... to the screen image of a "tou... man".

Article # 52. Amitabh's plea to donate blood (as transcribed from the article)

Gifting blood is one of the noblest gestures one can do for fellow beings. Although the blood so donated always goes to save the life of an unnamed patient, irrespective of age, sex, religion, status or color, the donor might not be aware of his contribution in saving a life.

"Nineteen bottles of blood saved my life", said Amitabh Bachchan in a message of appreciation sent to the Federation of Bombay Blood Banks. Among other things, Amitabh Bachchan owed his life to timely blood transfusion.

In a message to the All India Voluntary blood donation day, being observed on Friday throughout the country, the matinee idol also appealed to the citizens to donate blood voluntarily so that the life of those in need of blood could be saved.

Apart from organizing blood donation drives, the Federation strives to focus public attention on this day on the benefits of voluntary blood donations as opposed to commercial donations (sic) in blood. Blood banks affiliated to the Federation, including those of Municipal and Government hospitals are run on voluntarily donated blood which meets only about 20 percent of Bombay's requirement.

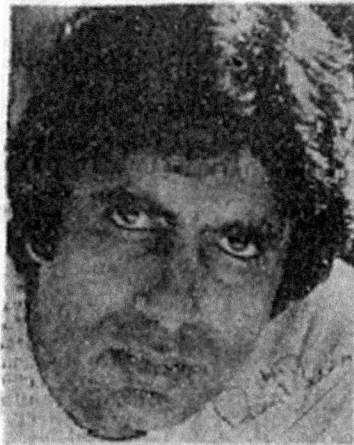

Amitabh plea to donate blood 52

By A Staff Reporter

Gifting blood is one of the noblest gestures one can do for fellow beings. Although the blood so donated often goes to save the life of an unarmed patient, irrespective of age, sex, religion, status or colour, the donor might not be aware of his contribution in saving a life.

"Nineteen bottles of blood saved my life," says Amitabh Bachchan in a message of appreciation sent to the Federation of Bombay Blood Banks. Among other things, Amitabh Bachchan owed his life to timely blood transfusion.

In a message to the All-India Voluntary blood donation day, being observed on Friday throughout the country, the matinee idol also appealed to the citizens to donate blood voluntarily so that the life of those in need of blood could be saved.

Apart from organising blood donation drives, the Federation strives to focus public attention on this day on the benefits of voluntary blood donation as opposed to commercialisation in blood.

Blood banks affiliated to the Federation, including those of Municipal and Government hospitals are run on voluntarily donated blood which meets only about 70 per cent of Bombay's requirements.

Article # 53. Save Amitabh Run

Arvind Pandya, a resident of Baroda completed a 550 Kilometre stretch of running backward on his 'Save Amitabh Run' reached Siddhi Vinayak Temple, in Bombay. He had vowed to do the run, backward, to Bombay if Mr. Bachchan recovered completely.

After reaching the temple, Arvind went straight to Amitabh's bungalow in Juhu-VileParle, where he was received by Amitabh himself, in the presence of a large audience.

Mrs. Jaya Bachchan tied a 'Rakhi' on Arvind's wrist as a token of gratitude towards the dedicated fan.

(Tying of Rakhi is symbolic of forming a sister-brother connection between women and men who are not blood relatives)

Arvind Pandya, who ran backwards all the way from Baroda, on a "Save Amitabh run," on his way to Sidhi Vinayak Mandir, Prabhadevi on Saturday morning. Report on Page 5.

'Save Amitabh run' 53

By A Staff Reporter

Arvind Pandya a resident of Baroda completed a 550 km. stretch of running backward on his "Save Amitabh run" on Saturday morning on reaching Sidhi Vinayak Mandir, Prabhadevi.

Arvind, who is a great fan of filmstar Amitabh Bachchan had vowed to do the run back upto Bombay if Mr. Bachchan recovered completely.

From Sidhi Vinayak Mandir, Prabhadevi Arvind went straight to Amitabh's bungalow in Juhu-Vile Parle, where he was received by the filmstar himself, in the presence of a large audience.

Mrs. Jaya Bachchan, reportedly tied a rakhi on Arvind's wrist as a token of gratitude towards the dedicated fan.

Mr. Pandya was accompanied all the way by two cyclist and a motorcyclist.

Amitabh Bachchan, a few days before he was hurt, "I'll be 50 in ten years time. I don't look the way I'm looking now, I won't have the same body, same mind, not even the same voice...There'll be some else who's younger, better looking."

July 1982, Article # 40

Premonition?

A few days before he was hurt, Amitabh was quoted as saying, "I'll be 50 in ten years' time. I don't look the way I am looking now. I won't have the same body, the same mind, not even the same voice. There'll be someone else, who is younger, better looking "

At the beginning of 1982, Amitabh suffered a serious bout of Asthma in Delhi.

This forced him to cut down his hectic schedule of working up to three shifts a day, so the superstar had spent the last few months before this accident, completing existing projects and undertaking no new ones.

As a result, when he had this accident, Amitabh had only two incomplete films on the sets, *Coolie* and Ramesh Bahl's *Pukaar*. Ramesh Sippy's *Shakti* was already complete, *Nastik* was completed except for the dubbing, and *Andha Kanoon* which featured Amitabh in a guest appearance, had only a few scenes to be shot.

For a film industry which had come to depend on Amitabh as its only instantly saleable name, the stake in the actor was much greater than just an immediate matter of blocked finances. Leading producer Prakash Mehra had planned two films around him *Sharabi* and *Kayaar*, Ramesh Sippy was already planning his next venture *Shatranj* with Amitabh in the lead.

Director Raj Sippy has cast him for *Taala Chaabi* and Amjad Khan and a host of other producers were reportedly waiting for him to start signing films once again.

The doctors had predicted a minimum of six-month convalescence and possibly a whole year off work for the star, it was clear that most producers would have to hold their horses.

According to Amitabh's brother Ajitabh and his wife Ramola, the public perception of the superstar as a kind, loving father and gentleman is both accurate and richly deserved.

"With Amitabh, it is also a national thing. He is everyone's brother, father, son."

A close friend, Yash Johar said emphatically "But this delay means nothing at all, anybody can afford to wait eight to ten months with a man like Amitabh in your movie. Today he has reduced the number of movies in hand, but in the past he has been ill for three and four months at a time when he used to sign ten times the number of films, and nothing happened to anybody."

At West End hotel Bangalore, a few days before the incident, July 1982

At the opening of the Supper Room, West End Hotel, Bangalore, chief guest, film star Amitabh Bachchan (centre) is seen with officials of the hotel (from left) Mr. Dominic, Mr. Raghavan, Mr. K. P. Kannampilly, Maimuna Tulsi, Priya Mascarenhas, Gen. D. C. Misra, and Mrs. and Mr. Ketan Desai.

This picture was taken at the opening of the Supper room, at the grand West End Hotel, Bangalore where Amitabh was the chief guest. Amitabh was also staying at this hotel during his *Coolie* filming days.

Seen in the picture are (from left) Mr. Dominic, Mr. Raghavan, Mr. K. P. Kannampilly, Ms. Maimuna Tulsi, Ms. Priya Mascarenhas, General D.C. Misra, Mrs. Kanchan Desai and Mr. Ketan Desai.

A brief mention of two officials from the picture:

West End's Technical Director, Mr. K.P. Kannampilly (third from left) later set-up his own luxury chain of hotels & resorts brand, 'The Fern' and 'The Fern Residency'. The company is known for their pioneering leadership in carbon reduction in their hotels, winning awards for Eco-Innovation. They have been leading environmentally sensitive hotels, employing sustainable systems and technologies for resource and emission reduction measures on-site.

West End's Marketing Director, Priya Mascarenhas (fifth from left) is now a businesswoman but she champions the cause for greenery, working tirelessly in raising awareness, stating that curative powers of nature cannot be replaced with any other. Priya's boutique garden has won accolades and trophies for years, including 'The Most Outstanding Ornamental Garden' of Bengaluru award.

A brief history of The West End Hotel:

The West End hotel is Bangalore city's most iconic and oldest surviving hotel, completing 131 years of operation in 2018. The West End first started in 1887 as the English Gentlemen's Lodge, run by the Bronson couple and then in 1912 was taken over by the Spencers. The Taj West End, as it is now known, was leased by the Taj group in 1984 for 99 years.

Over the years, The West End has seen patronage of Indian Royalty, British Aristocracy, Hollywood and Bollywood celebrities enjoying the luxurious hospitality and old-world graciousness. Among its esteemed patrons have been Sir Winston Churchill, Prince Charles, Dame Peggy Ashcroft and Rex Harrison.

David Lean extensively shot his 'Passage to India' film here.

I had an occasion to stay at the Taj West End in January 2017. Bangalore (now Bengaluru) city has changed tremendously over the decades, but the Taj West End has retained its charm and hospitality of the bygone era. It was exactly like its pictures from earlier years.

Once within the hotel precincts, I found it to be still misty, magical and full of its 1887 charm. It enveloped me as soon as I entered the hotel. The grand arches open up to a majestic reception and as I walked through its lush green environs, I was taken into an era of the past, stumbling along pieces of history. I could feel the peace and serenity, could hear the silent whispers of romance, of time standing still as I walked through its corridors through to the interior.

It was a beautiful and unforgettable visit for me.

There were many articles talking about theories, rumors and exploring possible causes for an incident that virtually brought an entire nation to a standstill. One such article is reproduced here, written by world-renowned, revered astrologer, prophesier, and columnist Bejan Daruwalla. He is known to combine the principles of Vedic and Western astrology. Bejanji has won numerous accolades and widespread recognition for his unerring predictions.

Amitabh—Libra, stress & strain

By Bejan Daruwalla

FRANTIC phone call, innumerable letters, a thousand inquiries a day for the health of Libran film star, Amitabh Bachchan, has resulted in the writing of this very special piece on Librans in general and Amitabh in particular. After all, Mrs. Indira Gandhi took time off to visit Amitabh. It was in a way a salute to the film industry. Also a deep concern and involvement with the October 11-born lanky star. And, in any case I am not yet through with the series on stress and strain the astrological way. Perhaps it is the Ahmedabadi way of killing five birds with half a stone.

"There's great disparity between modern and ancient astrologers, specially the Chaldeans, about the Libra sun-sign. The moderns call you charming, diplomatic, easy-going and excellent company. The Chaldeans dub you as war-like, selfish, self-oriented, and self-indulgent.

What's the truth? For that, you should know and understand that Libra is the 7th sign of Zodiac. The 7th sign stands for both marriage and war. The modern astrologers emphasise the marriage aspect; the Chaldeans, the war angle. My personal belief is that, you Libra, show your aggression on the intellectual plane in areas of public affairs, marriage, foreign matters. Therefore, to me it is self-evident that, Libra makes a good lawyer, a fine advocate of public causes, an excellent general, a superb statesman, a quote from my own Libra horoscope, Orient paperbacks.

Is it not ironical and yet very valid that Amitabh, the dhisum-dhisum hero, was knocked out by a screen blow that has repercussions and hospitalisation in real life? A clear case of a Libran paradox! The health hazards of Libra are best summarised as under:—

"The complaints of Libra are gravel, stone, pains in the back, inflammation of the kidneys and bladder, general debility. When there are afflictions from the sign Libra, the blood loses its alkaline properties and a physical condition known as over-acidity results. This affects the stomach causing flatulency, affects the sweat glands, causing unpleasant body odours, weakens the kidneys leading to various forms of kidney disease and finally affects the lower brain leading to hallucinations and insanity.

The herbs of Libra then must tone the kidneys, keep the pores of the skin active that the daily load of carbonaceous waste material may be lessened, and restore the sodium phosphate the mineral salt which helps to maintain the balance between acids and alkalis.

Some of the herbs of Libra are to be found in every district where human life is possible, the following being the most common:—

Pennyroyal—which is warming and soathing. Many mothers use a weak tea of this herb for feverish, teething babies.

Violet—this is recognised as a remedy for internal and external cancer, a disease condition which always indicates lack of the phosphates. It has a cooling effect on the kidneys and giddiness arising from nervous kidneys.

Feverfew—will strengthen and cleanse the kidneys.

Catmint—is similar to Pennyroyal and Feverfew in its action.

Silverweed—is usual where this is over-activity of the kidneys but this should be used cautiously and combined with a herb of an emollient nature.

Archangel—will open the pores of the skin. Bearberry—is a kidney tonic but should be used only with the milder herbs.

Burdock—may be safely used in all forms of kidney weakness.

Yes, all these has been lifted from a Ceylonese astrologer.

I can hear the readers shouting, "all this is very well, Bejan, but tell us about the fate of our darling Amitabh!" It was on July 26, that Amitabh suffered a grievous injury which laid him low. By western astrology Saturn-Mars were in Libra. On the 26th, Saturn was conjoined with Moon. Saturn is the planet of death destruction. The moon symbolises the mind. No wonder it was such a close call.

As long as Saturn remains in Libra by western astrology, Amitabh will not be out of total danger. This also means that Librans in general will feel stress and strain as long as Saturn continues the sojourn in Libra. Saturn gets out of Libra only on November 28, 1982. Therefore, whether it be Amitabh, or other Librans, they will heave a real sigh of relief only from December 1, 1982. Not before.

This piece is not a paean of praise on Librans. It is all about stress and strains. Though the Libran is very often a private person, he cannot live without company, very specially a free and happy exchange of ideas and opinions. This is not always possible. Discord and disharmony is a fact of human existence. The Libran would like to forget it. Alas, that's not possible. This will create psychological problems and psycho-somatic diseases.

The wisest policy for Librans is to strike the safe middle course, namely, "Medio tutissiumus ibis". The reason is that Libra, the sign of scales, always tries to see both the sides of the question and therefore falls between two stools."

Amitabh – Libra, stress & strain. By Bejan Daruwala (as transcribed from the article)

FRANTIC phone call, innumerable letters, thousands of inquiries a day for the health of Libran film star Amitabh Bachchan, has resulted in the writing of this very special piece on Librans in general and Amitabh in particular. After all, Mrs. Indira Gandhi took time off to visit Amitabh. It was in a way a salute to the film industry. Also a deep concern and involvement with the October 11 born lanky star. And, in any case, I am not yet through with the series on stress and strain the astrological way. Perhaps it is the Ahmedabadi way killing five birds with half a stone.

"There's great disparity between modern and ancient astrologers, specially the Chaldeans, about the Libra sun-sign. The modern calls you charming, diplomatic, easy going and excellent company. The Chaldeans dub you as war-like, selfish, self-oriented and self-indulgent.

What's the truth? For that, you should know and understand that Libra is the 7th sign of Zodiac. The 7th sign stands for both marriage and war. The modern astrologer emphasizes the marriage aspect; the Chaldeans, the war angle. My personal belief is that, you Libra, show your aggression on the intellectual plane in areas of public affairs, marriage, foreign matters. Therefore, to me it is self –evident that, Libra makes a good lawyer, a fine advocate of public causes, an excellent general, a superb statesman, a quote from my own Libra horoscope. Orient paperbacks.

It is not ironical and yet very valid that Amitabh, the dhishum-dhishum hero, was knocked out by a screen blow that has repercussions and hospitalization in real life? A clear case of a Libra paradox!

The health hazards of Libra are the best summarized as under:-

"The complaints of Libra are gravel stones, pains in the back, inflammation of the kidneys and bladder, general debility. When there are afflictions from under the sign

Libra, the blood loses its alkaline properties and a physical condition known as over acidity results, this affects the stomach causing flatulency, affects the sweat glands, causing unpleasant body odors, weakens the kidney leading to various forms of kidney disease and finally affects the lower brain leading to hallucinations and insanity.

The herbs of Libra then must tone the kidneys, keep the pores of the skin active that the daily load of carbonaceous waste material may be lessened, and restore the sodium phosphates, the mineral salt which helps to maintain the balance between the acids and alkalis.

Some of the herbs of Libra are to be found in every district where human life is possible, the following being the most common:-

Pennyroyal - which is warming and soothing, many mothers use a weak tea of this herb for feverish, teething babies.

Violet – this is recognized as a remedy for internal and external cancer, a disease condition which always indicates lack of the phosphates, It has a cooling effect on the kidneys and giddiness arising from nervous kidneys.

Feverfew - will strengthen and cleanse the kidneys.

Silverweed – is usual where this is fewer activity of the kidneys this but this should be used cautiously and combined with a herb of an emollient future.

Archangel – will open the pores of the skin. Bearberry – is a kidney tonic but should be used only with the milder herbs.

Burdock – may be safely be used in all forms of kidneys weakness.

Yes, all these has been lifted form a Ceylonese astrologer.

I can hear the readers shouting, "All this is very well, Bejan, but tell us about the fate of our darling Amitabh!" It was on July 26 (24), that Amitabh suffered a grievous injury which laid him low. By western astrology Saturn – Mars were in Libra. On the 26th, Saturn was conjoined with the moon. Saturn is the planet of death destruction. The moon symbolizes the mind. No wonder it was such a close call.

As long as Saturn remains in Libra by western astrology, Amitabh will not be out of total danger. This also means that Librans in general will feel stress and strain as long as Saturn continues the sojourn in Libra. Saturn gets out of Libra only on November 28, 1982. Therefore, whether it be Amitabh, or other Librans, they will have a real sigh of relief only from December 1, 1982. Not before.

This piece is not a paean of praise on Librans. It is all about stress and strains. Though the Libran is very often a private person, he cannot live without company, very specially a free and happy exchange of ideas and opinions. This is not always possible. Discord and disharmony is a fact of human existence. The Libran would like to forget it. Alas, that's not possible. This will create psychological problems and psycho-somatic diseases.

The wisest policy for Librans is to strike the safe middle course, namely. "Medio tutissiumus ibis". The reason is that Libra, the sign of scales, always tries to see both the sides of the question and therefore falls between two stools.

"Felled by a punch in the film Coolie, almost dead....got up, survived, recovered and started again from where I left off....punching the punch that brought me down...!! Get up and fight!! Never give UP!"

FACEBOOK.COM/AMITABHBACHCHAN/

2.8.82

I WAVE NOW AFTER 1982, EACH SUNDAY.. THE WAVE IS THE SAME
THE PEOPLE ARE THE SAME, THE SENTIMENT IS THE SAME ..
BLESSED I AM FOR THIS .. BLESSED ARE YOU WHO REMAIN WITH ME ..

The album cover for Amitabh's show, 'Live Tonite Amitabh Bachchan with Kalyanji Anandji'.

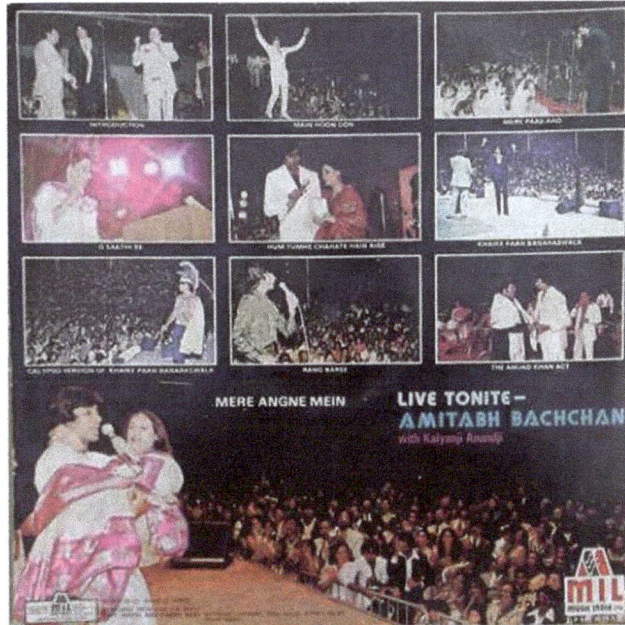

Below pictures are actually postcards I had purchased, with Amitabh's autograph, but I never sent them to anybody as I was not ready to part with them.

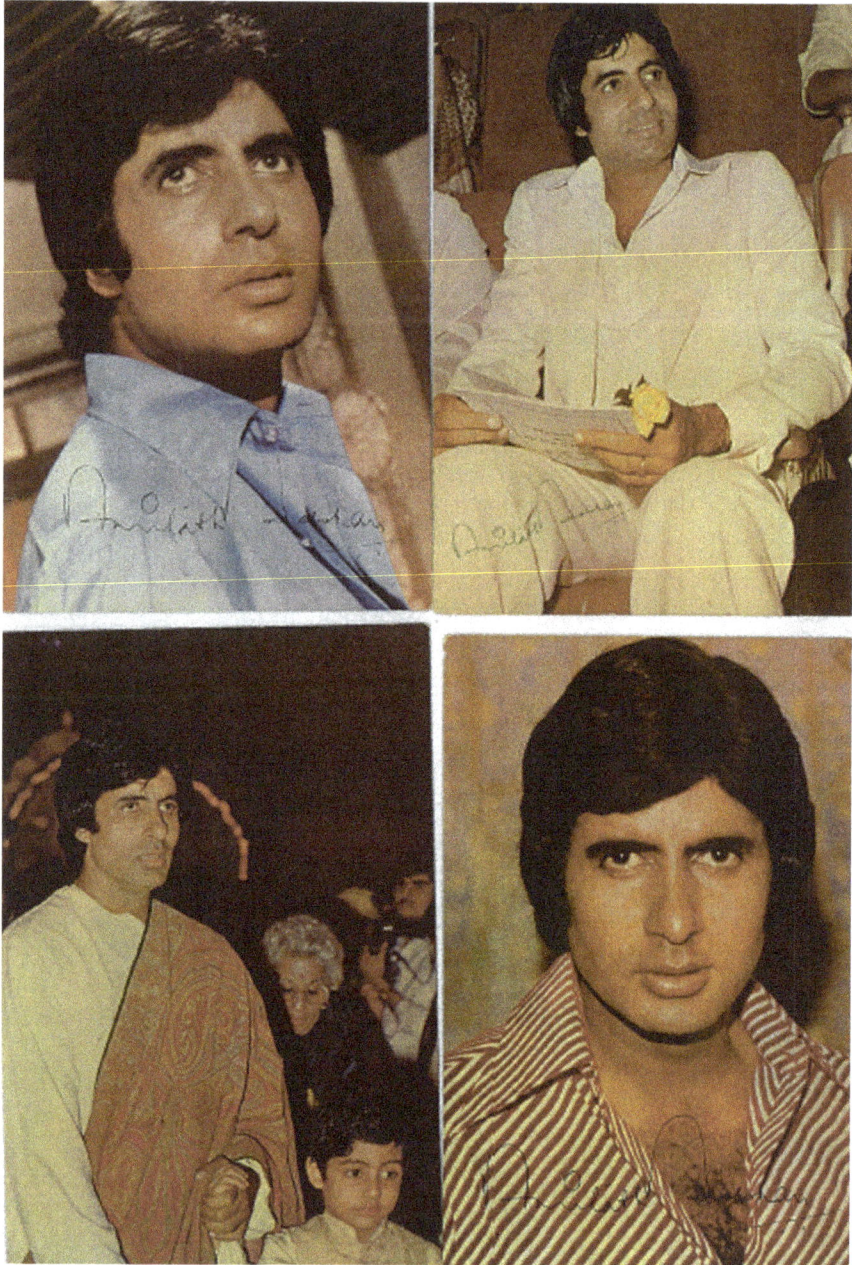

Amitabh with wife Jaya and his children, Shweta and Abhishek.

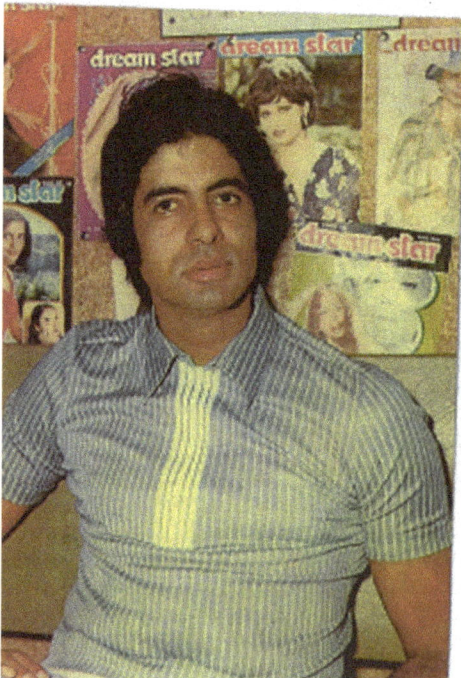

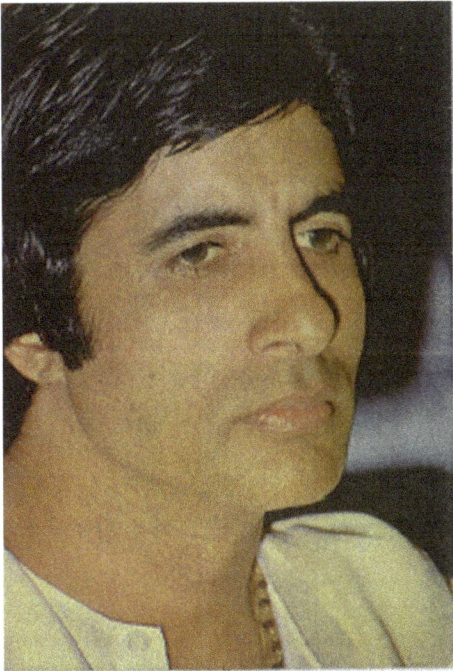

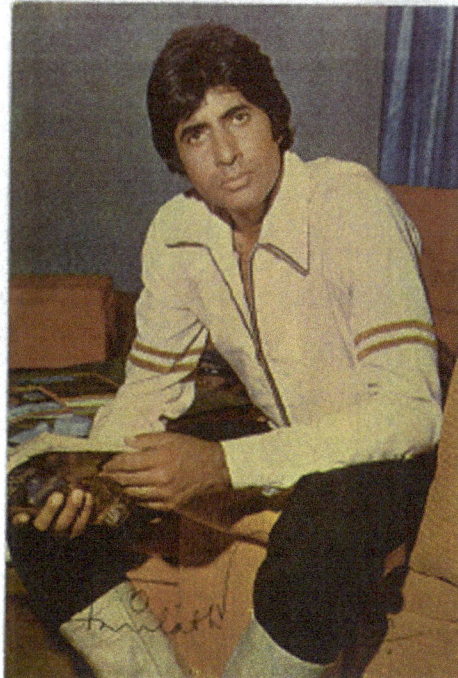

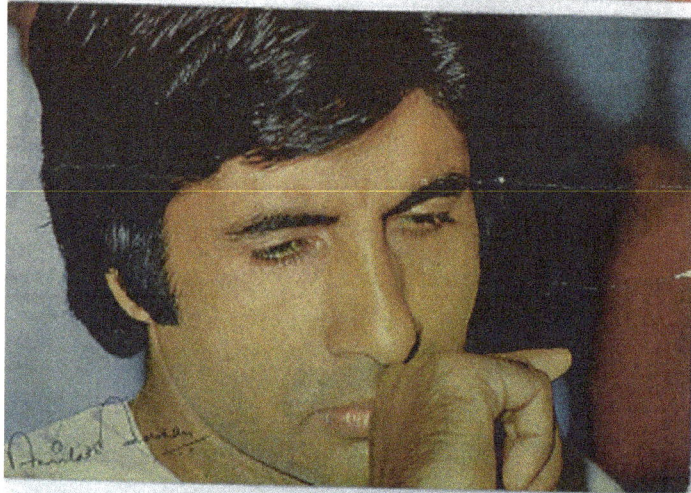

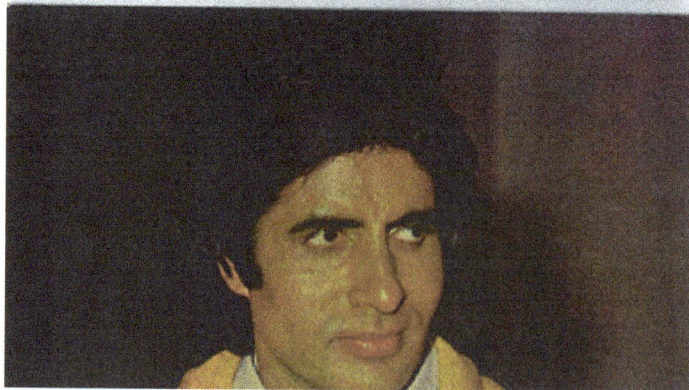

THE COMEBACK

Commencing work after the accident

Amitabh defied time and science, recovered speedily and resumed shooting on 7th January 1983. This was barely three months after leaving the hospital and a full nine months before doctors thought that he should ideally start work.

Amitabh Bachchan. Facebook

Amitabh and Jaya visited Bangalore as a thanksgiving pilgrimage. They visited temples, mosques, and churches to express their gratitude to all those who had worked around the clock to save his life.

"Before I started my work in Madras, I wanted to come here and express my thanks to you all for making my recovery possible." Amitabh Bachchan said while strolling down the corridors of St. Philomena's Hospital in Bangalore. Examining the bed on which he had lingered between life and death only a few months earlier, he asked the hospital staff: "How was I lying there? Which side was my head on? I hardly remember anything…"

Amitabh first went for a special 'pooja' to a Ganesha temple and then to the Raja Rajeswari Temple. The Tiruchi Swamigal blessed the actor as the Swami had earlier blessed via telephone, predicting a speedy recovery.

Going around the 'ashram' followed by a flock of devotees, Amitabh showed us once again, what human icons are made of. He chatted with the ashram staff, posed for photographs, obliged autograph hunters. Noticing a young lad with a plastered arm in a sling making his way through the crowd. Amitabh penned a 'get well' message on his cast.

It was a pilgrimage that left an everlasting impression on the minds of both the revered hero and his ardent fans.

Friday, 2nd December 1983, Movie *"Coolie"* released

This was the fight scene with his co-star where he was injured, but the injury was not due to the punch, but rather on the jump being mistimed while landing on the table, and due to this mistiming, the actor hit the corner of the table, instead of landing on top of it as he was meant to be.

In the final edit, the fight sequence between Amitabh Bachchan and Puneet Issar was frozen at a certain point and a superimposed message marked it as the exact moment when Amitabh was injured. Manmohan Desai did this edit on the suggestion of Amitabh Bachchan.

Puneet Issar met filmmaker Manmohan Desai on the sets of *Naseeb*. The filmmaker wanted to record something and was looking for a martial arts artiste with a good voice. Yash Johar, who was a friend of Puneet's father, director Sudesh Issar, took him to Desai, who was impressed with not just Puneet's baritone and a black belt, but also his personality and perfect-10 physique, and decided to cast him as the main villain in his next film, *Coolie*.

Puneet, an experienced stuntman, was to punch Amitabh in the stomach. Amitabh was required to spin around from the blow and fall heavily on a steel table. In his usual dare-devil style, Amitabh refused to let a double take over and did the scene himself.

Amitabh never blamed his co-star Puneet for this incident and put it down to an 'unfortunate accident' but the poor guy had to deal with the trauma of having landed the punch and the public vilification for a long while. It was believed that he got death threats while Amitabh was in the hospital and had to go underground for a while. After that, he was pretty much unemployable till he landed a big role as 'Duryodhan' in the TV Series "Mahabharat"

The film's ending was also altered due to Amitabh's grievous injury. The original script had Amitabh Bachchan die after Kader Khan shot him. But in the later edit, Manmohan Desai decided to change the ending. The Director, Manmohan Desai made the changes as he thought that it would have a negative impact on the audience, citing that Amitabh already recovered from a near-fatal injury at that time.

The modified ending had the protagonist recover after his operation, just like he had done in real life. It would be inappropriate for the man who had cheated death for real not to do so on screen, the director said.

The blockbuster film *Coolie* was among the rare movies which crossed Rs. One crore (10 million) in earnings per territory. Till 1984, there were only thirteen such movies that grossed so much and Amitabh starred in nine of them. Despite the film's box office success and the wave of awards and hits that followed, Amitabh took a sabbatical from films in 1984 to enter politics in support of his long-time family friend, Rajiv Gandhi. Amitabh was elected to India's parliament when he contested the seat of Allahabad in 1984 and won by an overwhelming majority. His political career, however, was short-lived as he was not cut out for the wiliness, shrewdness and peculiar intricacies of India's political environment during those times. He resigned from his seat in 1989 and chose to end his political career.

This period also marked a slow downturn for his film career as only a handful of his movies were released and they performed poorly at the box office. Amitabh, who had just turned 50, then went into a self-imposed exile from films from 1992 to 1997.

Amitabh's dream – ABCL

It was during his break from acting that Amitabh set up "Amitabh Bachchan Corporation Limited" (ABCL) in 1995, a company to be involved in film production, distribution, TV software, audio, event management and allied profiles.

As a visionary businessman, Amitabh was way ahead of his time. It could also be that his venture was just too ambitious. Amitabh gave his company everything that he had: his brand, his contacts, his reputation and his money. Armed with all this showbiz arsenal the company planned for an events division, a film distribution division, and television content production, everything at once. He dreamt of bringing professionalism to the Bombay film industry, but ABCL was not successful. Suffering disaster after disaster, including the 1996 Miss World pageant, the company went bankrupt.

This was 1996 and Amitabh was 54. He was the sole breadwinner of his family, his daughter was about to be married into a reputable wealthy family, and his son had yet to start earning. And he had just lost absolutely everything in a massive public business failure.

When his dream turned sour and the company went bankrupt, Amitabh made a return to the silver screen to revive his sagging fortunes.

His "comeback" movie flopped, which was unheard of. An Amitabh movie hadn't flopped since 1973. What made this move worse was Amitabh was also the producer for this movie. It impacted his star power and further damaged his bank account. The next movie did not do well either, or the next, or the next. Between 1996 and 2000 there were seven box office flops. Some of them did do reasonably well, but none of them came close to the numbers that an "Amitabh" movie was expected to do.

Amitabh's comeback did not work out well. Critics and fans alike rejected him as an also-ran. He had been dragged through several lawsuits for failing to repay the company's debt. In fact, the actor admitted that he was forced to do his first commercial for BPL and later, for several other brands, to pay off his massive debt.

Advertising gigs were mostly for newcomers who were looking to get a foothold in the film industry. Brand endorsement was not a "respectable' option for film stars. It would also mean a silver screen megastar would have to accept a 'demotion' into the smaller world of advertising.

This was a very risky move for Amitabh as entering the advertising world after being a superstar in Bollywood was considered a downgrade. But this was the resilient and resourceful Amitabh. This was the time when he decided: "No job was too small to do" and he accepted the offer to do commercials.

Amitabh transformed the small world of advertising and brought the same commitment and professionalism to his ad campaigns that he did to his acting roles. Suddenly, the whole advertising world wasn't "beneath" the film industry. Other film actors followed suit, making brand endorsement a profitable alternative income source for many and a 'celebrated' thing to do.

Speaking on the debacle ABCL faced soon after its 1995 launch, Mr. Bachchan said the errors of the past centered around the bad management of the company. The marriage of the relatively new area of the entertainment business with professional managers went awry. These managers turned out to be green horns in understanding the business of entertainment, he said.

On 11th October 2003, the superstar celebrated his 61st birthday by re-launching his "sick" entertainment company ABCL as AB Corp. After paying the company's staggering debt, Amitabh had started talking extensively about reviving the company.

In an interview, Amitabh had once said: "We were five years ahead of time. There was no experience of how to run the business of entertainment. There was mismanagement and too much reliance on executives."

"In 1995, I started what was ABCL, which was going to encompass the entire entertainment vision that we were growing into. We started well but we ran into trouble. The company went bankrupt and instead of closing the company down, against a lot of wishes of our advisers, I chose to keep it alive and worked hard to pay back all our debts and get the company back on its feet again. I'm happy to say that after having taken care of that, with a lot of trouble, lot of assistance from friends and well-wishers, we are now back on our feet. But having learnt some bitter lessons in the sphere of management of entertainment companies, we decided that we would start taking very small steps forward."

Speaking on the near-bankruptcy of his entertainment company, Amitabh said, "My friends from the business world told me that entrepreneurship wasn't my cup of tea. But having got into it, we at AB Corp Limited are determined to tide over the crisis. I was advised to shut down the company and get on with my life. But I've not acceded to the urgings of my well-wishers because I believe in the original vision of my company."

Amitabh had every intention of living up to his corporate commitments. "Even if I have to scrub floors, I'll do so to pay back the money I owe the creditors. I never said I wouldn't pay them back."

The Return to Glory

And then came a television show which made history. And so the man rose again, like a phoenix, and captivated a nation.

The superstar remembers how the reality show "Kaun Banega Crorepati" (KBC) changed his life and pulled him out of his financial crunch. The 'Big B' posted on his blog, "Ten years ago in the year 2000, when the entire world was celebrating the new century, I was celebrating my disastrous fortune. There were no films, no money, no company, a million legal cases against me and the tax authorities had put notice of recovery on my home… An offer for television changed all that when I agreed to anchor KBC much against all the advice and resentment from friends, family, and advisers."

"I merely sat back and played the game as best it could be played".

Television in India was considered a poor second cousin to films. Cable television network had yet to take off and it was still fairly early days of satellite TV revolution in India. Channel content and TV serials were only just gaining mass popularity. There were some big series that were successful but they were mainly in the genre of family drama or epic religious production. Television was still considered small time; especially a television game show. And especially for a star as reputable, dignified, and talented as Amitabh!

The first episode of KBC was aired on Star Plus on 3 July 2000. The living rooms of Indian households were filled with emotion and a surreal euphoric sensation. Here was their matinee idol, live in front of hundreds of real people in the television studios and engaging with everyone from all walks of life. This was their superstar in soul-stirring conversations with them, listening to their life stories and gripping narratives. It had all of India glued to their television sets. Their 'angry young man' idol of yesteryear was now their stylish and suave quiz master and a benevolent authority figure.

Though the episodes which aired in 2000 were a huge hit, it wasn't good news for everyone. The show was blamed for a slump in attendance at the country's cinemas. The cinema owners complained that "there was a significant dip in collections on the days the show is aired. The 6 pm and 9 pm shows are the worst hit... Amitabh Bachchan has such a magnetic, compelling personality. A lot of people just watch the show to be able to see him perform. Nobody is interested in coming to the theatres to watch movies when the game show is on."

This was the game changer in Amitabh Bachchan's life. He desperately needed a winner to prove a point to those of his critics who had written him off as a spent force. For many years, his die-hard fans had waited for that dream film, their favorite hero's comeback vehicle. But a string of failures in the 1990s had ensured that the wait continued.

With KBC, Amitabh was able to warm his way back into Indian hearts and became the 'Shahenshah' (Emperor) of Indian showbiz once again.

The dreams and fortunes of many other Bollywood directors hoped to cash in on Amitabh Bachchan's newfound return to superstardom. The entirety of Bollywood was waiting with baited breath to see if the aging showman could also bring the smiles back to an ailing Mumbai film industry.

As wife Jaya observes: "His commitments are more emotional than real...His best I feel is yet to come...His potential after 30 years remains untapped...His best will come only when he works with a director who thinks exactly like him."

Following his resurrection as a showman par excellence with the phenomenal success of KBC, and the subsequent resounding success of *Mohabbatein*, Amitabh was all set to shine once again on the silver screen.

With the success of KBC, Amitabh had finally returned to his former glory.

Today, he has a slew of films in his kitty that marked the return of the legend - a comeback trail continuing through into 2018. This is a feat that has eluded many stars not just in India, but around the world.

Amitabh's daughter, Shweta Bachchan Nanda, on her Dad's 73rd birthday: "He is now 73. His popularity has stood the test of time—many smear campaigns, a brief encounter with politics (which he regrets until this day), a near-fatal accident, a greying goatee, and a change of address. His arena of work is like a gladiator's pit; it's you against the beasts, and if you manage to end the day alive then glory is yours. The only caveat is that you have to get back in the pit and get ready to fight, to prove yourself yet again, another day".

Kaun Banega Crorepati journey: From 2000 to 2018

Kaun Banega Crorepati (KBC) originally aired on Star Plus for the first three Seasons from 2000 to 2007 and then on Sony TV for six Seasons since 2010.

The magic, power, and reach of KBC show combined with the style, elan, and talent of Amitabh not only changed the fortunes of Star TV and Sony India, but also made careers and created employment in the overall media & entertainment sector. The show and the host are still breaking viewership records and ruling prime-time charts. The number of viewers and revenues have grown exponentially with each season. The show has also been credited with bringing a technology-based show to Indian television at a time when even owning a mobile phone was considered luxurious. The recent KBC Season 9 has taken the adoption of technology and the Government's digital initiative further by foregoing the practice of writing winner's cheques and instead, doing payments via digital transfer.

Season 1: 2000–01: KBC premiered on 3 July 2000 and was hosted by Amitabh Bachchan, his first appearance on Indian television.

Season 2: 2005–06: After a four-year hiatus, on 5th August 2005, the show was restarted, renamed as KBC 2 with Amitabh as the host. After shooting for 61 of the 85 scheduled episodes, Amitabh fell ill. He was to return after his recovery, but his ill-health prevented him from filming the remaining 24 episodes. The shoes of Amitabh were too big to fill and the channel decided to take the show off the air as a temporary measure.

Season 3: 2007: For KBC 3 commencing on 22nd January 2007, the channel brought on Superstar Shahrukh Khan to host this season. The show started off well but then ratings began to drop significantly due to various factors and so this season ended on 19 April 2007 with a special finale.

Season 4: 2010: The fourth season, KBC 4 brought back the original host, Amitabh Bachchan. The show very significantly started on 11 October 2010, on Amitabh's 68th birthday, with four shows every week, airing 36 episodes.

Season 5: 2011: Amitabh was now the very popular host for this highly rated show and returned to host the fifth season which started on 15 August 2011 through to 17 November 2011 airing four episodes a week from Monday to Thursday.

Season 6: 2012–13: Amitabh continued as the host for the sixth season too, which premiered on 7 September 2012, but due to its growing popularity, it was now moved to prime time from Friday to Sunday evenings, with the season ending on 26 January 2013.

Season 7: 2013: The popularity of the show and Amitabh as the host continued through the seventh season, which commenced on 6 September 2013, on prime time from Friday to Sunday evenings.

Season 8: 2014: By now, Amitabh had become synonymous with the show and it was no surprise that he was hosting this season too. The series premiered on 17 August 2014 running through to 6 November 2014.

Season 9: 2017: KBC returned to air on 28 August 2017 with Amitabh continuing as the host. The show ended on 7 November 2017 and this time with 19.8 million registrations, the show made it to the top of TRP ratings in the Indian television industry.

Season 10: 2018: Preparations are on for the tenth season, where Amitabh will host the show. Registrations have commenced and the show will start airing from mid-August 2018 for a reportedly 60 episodes this season.

The Superstar

In hindsight, the foundations of Amitabh's second coming were firm. There was no stopping him. Amitabh was creating new parameters for how we judge someone to be a superstar with his image of the "Superstar of the Millennium." He has shown the world that he is not just a brilliant actor or a star but an institution in himself. His traits of professionalism, determination, and a never-say-die attitude are the differentiators that set him up for success and that have taken him this far.

There is a famous saying, used mostly in the Indian cricketing world: "Form is temporary. Class is permanent."

Applied to the world of films, we could extend the analogy to say that a film's success or failure does not determine the calibre of an actor. Yes, it does affect financial standing, and yes, it may drive future availability of work but no, it does not determine popularity with the audience and no, it does not affect a star's performance. An artiste rises above the movie and makes his impact known, with audience and critics alike.

It's a curious phenomenon that a man of such prodigious talents should also have possessed so much charisma. Nobody else had that combination. There was style, and polish and a great deal of seclusion which of course encouraged rumors, but this only augmented his aura. Any way you looked at it, the man exuded power.

There has only been one superstar in India, and that is Amitabh Bachchan. He is the complete entertainer, the one man industry who could conjure successes out of the most unlikely of films. That's amazing charisma! Combine this with his acting prowess, his histrionics ability, his singing, his comic timing, on-screen expressions of controlled rage, intense anger and silent passion and we are talking of a powerhouse, an absolute dynamo!

Superstars are made when legend overtakes the person. Only one superstar in India has seen his image rise higher in the sky even as his own fortunes have tumbled. Setbacks don't matter; it's the strength of character and the will to succeed that prevails. Not to sound clichéd, but it's true: When the going gets tough, the tough get going!

In 2002, on his 60th birthday, in an exclusive interview with BBC's Sanjeev Srivastava, Amitabh said he still had a long way to go to reach the height of his profession.

"Every artist has a desire to play as many different roles as he can... I'd say that I'm still open to fresh ideas, fresh roles that may come my way and which will challenge my creativity." Amitabh described his life and career as "fulfilling" and "wonderful". Faced with the choice, he said, he would go through it all again - even the failures. His earliest films flopped at the box office and Amitabh admitted that he had had second thoughts about acting at that time.

"Whenever you have a failure in life, it's a depressing phase, it kind of sets you back and makes you want to think again and I was no different.

"I also felt that maybe I made a wrong choice or a wrong decision, maybe this is not the place for me. It would've been extremely embarrassing for me to get back to Calcutta to my old job.

"But somehow, you know, encouragement and support from the parents and the family just kept me going and things changed."

Amitabh said he had no plans to retire as "there is no retirement age for actors and performers unless the audience decides otherwise".

"It is only the audience that can make actors retire when they stop getting roles or their work isn't appreciated".

Actor Salman Khan's message to Amitabh Bachchan on his 75th birthday:

"Bachchan saab is the prime example of where hard work can take you. Even at his age, his dedication and passion towards work is incredible. He's one of the best actors we have and he's maintained his stardom for over four decades. That's no joke. I wish I was as hardworking as him. I'm just lucky."

Social Media Megastar

Making one young fan very happy by writing 'get well soon' on the child's cast, the star continues to build relationships with his fans. Amitabh connects with his fans across the world through social media platforms, responding to questions and well-wishes on Twitter (@SrBachchan) and through his official blog page http://srbachchan.tumblr.com/

With a combined count of more than 60 million followers on social media platforms, Amitabh Bachchan has completed a decade of writing his blog, through which he stays connected with what he calls his "extended family". He is one of the most active actors on social media in the world and does all the interaction himself, including writing posts, and acknowledging and replying to messages.

He fears when his writing does not garner much response from fans. "It is not just the continuity of my writings, it is also the continuity of your feelings as well when you do not respond. I fear there has been a loss. A loss is unbearable and so it remains constant," he said.

As per a post on Amitabh's blog, he handles his social media activity himself contrary to what others assume. "There is no substitute to personal attention and care, none. Long may this survive". He says the "harmony of togetherness" is the "ultimate celebration".

Through social media, he became the king of his reputation.

In his early years, he was always cooperative with the press. In fact, he always made an effort to be nice and pleasant to deal with. When he and Jaya decided to get married, he wrote to everyone he knew in the press asking them to come over that evening so that a pleasant surprise could be revealed. He didn't play games with the press, nor did he favor anyone in particular. Much earlier, in 1987, Amitabh once quoted, "I sometimes feel that I have been born to attract controversy. Whatever I do becomes controversial."

In the 1980s and 90s, 'Big B' to the outside world was ruthless, devastating in wit, irreverent about the press, impudent towards convention, and iconoclastic towards institutions. Few understood the humane vision that he articulated. A very personal man, Amitabh has often come across as arrogant to people because of his aloofness. His closest colleagues have commented how despite knowing Amitabh for decades, there is still a great distance between them, and how despite decades of friendship, he keeps his thoughts and his personal life to himself.

The real Amitabh, according to me, is courteous, kind, generous, shy rather than impudent, physically strong and courageous, yet rather timid and prudish in his relations with the world. However, much of the real Amitabh emerges in his private blog. You can find moments which show a warm, witty human being, sometimes sentimental, often selfless, always sincere.

The Global Contender

By 2000, Amitabh's brilliance was being recognized across nations. In June that year, he became the first living Asian to be modelled in wax at Madame Tussauds Wax Museum in London. In France, he received the highest civilian honor. In 2007, the Knight of the Legion of Honour was conferred upon him by the French Government for his exceptional career in the world of cinema and beyond.

In 2012, BBC News held an online poll where they asked for viewer's choice for the greatest star of stage or screen of the last thousand years. The results were declared in October 2012 and BBC News Online users chose Amitabh Bachchan as the winner. It was no contest. Mr. Amitabh Bachchan was voted in by a large margin. It was the first time an Indian film star was voted the greatest star of stage or screen by any online users' poll. Sir Laurence Olivier received second place, followed by Sir Alec Guinness in third.

To his fans, the crowning of Amitabh Bachchan as the millennium's biggest star was only a vindication of their long-held belief in their hero's prowess.

In an interview with the BBC, Amitabh said: "As a matter of fact, there has been a lot of disbelief and surprise as far as this announcement is concerned." Amitabh said it was a humbling experience to find one's name in the company of Hollywood greats like Laurence Olivier, Alec Guinness, and others.

He said if he had been asked to choose the star of the millennium, his vote would have gone to Marlon Brando.

"I can safely say that for myself and many others, there hasn't really been a single actor who came after him who was not influenced by him. His sheer strength and greatness of performance, his presence and style makes him my star of the millennium."

Amitabh has been consistently featuring in the top ten list of Forbes India Celebrity 100 list. A few years ago when Forbes.com released its list of the five most powerful Indian film stars, it wasn't any reigning heartthrob, but the legendary Amitabh Bachchan who came out on top. The list was compiled according to the Forbes 'proprietary formula' weighing salary, number of press clips returned on Lexis-Nexis, and by gauging popularity from searches on the Dow Jones interactive and Google.

The Government of India has awarded Amitabh with the highest civilian awards: the Padma Shri in 1984, the Padma Bhushan in 2001 and the Padma Vibhushan in 2015.

Amitabh is also a four-time National award winner for his films Agneepath in 1990, Black in 2005, Paa in 2009 and Piku in 2015. In all, Amitabh Bachchan has won 15 Filmfare awards, considered as the Oscars of Bollywood (the Hindi language film industry). With 41 nominations, he is also the most-nominated performer in a major acting category at Filmfare Awards.

Amitabh has featured in many advertising campaigns raising awareness over community problems, supporting and promoting various health-related issues in the country such as childhood immunization programme, tuberculosis, and the Clean India campaign.

In 2002, Amitabh was appointed as UNICEF goodwill ambassador for the polio eradication campaign in India and continues this association to this day. In 2014, Rotary International and World Health Organization declared India a polio-free country.

In 2014, United Nations appointed him as the UN Ambassador for Girl Child. This appointment is now extended till 2019 where Amitabh will be championing the cause of the measles and rubella infection inoculations.

In May 2017, the World Health Organization appointed Amitabh Bachchan as its goodwill ambassador for hepatitis to boost awareness and intensify action to arrest the epidemic in South-East Asia region. In accepting this appointment, Amitabh said, "I am absolutely committed to the cause of hepatitis. As a person living with hepatitis B, I know the pain and sufferings that hepatitis causes. No one should ever suffer from viral hepatitis."

In May 2018, Microsoft Co-founder Bill Gates acknowledged Amitabh's contribution in helping India become polio-free by being the face of the 'Pulse Polio Movement' and the social influencer in spearheading this campaign.

AMITABH - THE SURVIVOR

Mind over Matter

His accident, and the way the whole country reacted, including the then Prime Minister herself, vividly highlighted the unprecedented stature which Amitabh enjoyed. Amitabh remembers, "I know that I was and still am full of gratitude for the prayers and wishes of my fans, colleagues and fellow beings. Strangers, whom I'd never met and perhaps never will, had prayed, fasted and walked miles to see me. I was so overwhelmed that there was this constant burden in my heart of not knowing how to repay such warmth".

Amitabh jumped back into action within three months of leaving the hospital, displaying extraordinary willpower in getting his physical and emotional health back into shape. His super-fast turnaround was thanks to a combination of love and care from his family as well as adopting a disciplined regime. This ensured that Amitabh returned to his normal physiological and psychological state in an unusually short time. However, there were repercussions from the numerous procedures and surgeries that his body underwent in those two months, and it left him with a series of after effects.

He had two stomach surgeries in quick succession, leading to the development of two hernias in the lower abdomen. These hernias caused him sharp pains when standing too long or walking too much. During his dance and action scenes, the pain would intensify.

But did this stop him from acting or doing more films?

Of course not! Amitabh went on to do more films than ever before. For proof, simply take a look at all his films released post-1982.

It requires immense courage and resilience to continue in the face of health challenges. It does not matter how much one hurts on the inside or how much of a beating the body has taken, there is an unspoken pressure to maintain a façade of normalcy. When you are a star, you are constantly in the limelight, with an almost microscopic scrutiny. More so when you are a superstar and have acquired the persona of a strong authoritative figure. Amitabh's screen reputation as an 'angry young man' demanded that he project the image of a fit, healthy physique with a positive, optimistic demeanor to the outside world.

Every successful person, and especially the ones we tend to look to for inspiration in our own lives, have faced their fair share of setbacks before, during and after achieving success.

Amitabh has shown us through his actions and a positive attitude, how to 'accept' negative situations and turn them around into opportunities for improvement. He changed his approach from 'resisting what is' and instead focused on moving ahead with 'concrete actions' and adjusted his lifestyle to a new future. There was a renewed focus on establishing a regimen of exercise and controlled eating patterns.

"Struggles and uncertainties, successes and disappointments, accusations and controversies, ill health and months in hospital, all such a vivid kaleidoscope of moments, events, images, simply unbelievable and unimaginable," blogs Amitabh.

Riddled With Accidents

Accidents and ill health seem to haunt Amitabh.

1983: A year after the *Coolie* accident, while celebrating Diwali with his family in Delhi, Amitabh burnt his palms badly.

An innocuous looking fire-cracker went off like a bomb in his left hand. It was a spurious 'sparkling fountain', which exploded in his hand as he was lighting it.

In an instant, the left hand had melted into a fist shape, with nothing left of it. No fingers, no nails, no nothing. It was a horrific sight. The entire palm and the area below his wrist just disappeared, burnt almost into a pulp.

Everyone around him was shocked, unable to comprehend what had just happened! To witness a freak accident like this and see him lose his hand in an instant, it was just terrible for Amitabh and his family.

Amitabh was in the middle of shooting *Inquilab* at the time. His first thought was not for himself but for the film and its makers. How would he shoot? How would the film be completed? There was a deadline to be met. If not, it would impact the film's release date and cause the Producer to face big financial losses.

In the 1980s, the Indian film industry was not the commercialized, corporatized environment that it is today. Financial institutions and banks did not offer loans for movies nor were there insurance companies underwriting the films. It was all left to the individual producer to manage the risks and operate with their own funds, dealing with natural disasters and human accidents alike.

The immediate priority, however, was to get Amitabh to the hospital and into emergency surgery. The process of treatment turned out to be very complicated. Delicate procedures were undertaken to separate each finger from the melted mass. It was an intricate and very painful process and carried a huge amount of risk as one small slip would mean the loss of a finger or even function of the entire hand.

Because of Amitabh's very recent surgeries under general anesthesia, the doctors were reluctant to administer him another dose so soon. But sedative was required to perform the intricate work on his hand.

The deadline to complete shooting was looming and Amitabh was desperate to get back and not cause further delay. The doctors did not think that the hand would heal in time for him to get back to work. But Amitabh was stubborn. He asked them to do the best they could so he could get back to completing the film.

He suggested that the doctors perform surgery without 'knocking him out'. In other words, to do it while he was conscious and awake. Amitabh recalls, "I told them to do it live. When the pain became too unbearable, I would tell them to stop and continue the next day. After days of work on it and some basics being achieved, I sought leave and reported for work, hand in bandage. If you see the film, you will notice that I made a style statement of my left hand by wearing a handkerchief over it. All the work that followed was done with my hand covered with a handkerchief".

Amitabh's hand was taking too long to heal. The skin was still raw and even a gust of breeze on it would make him wince in pain. The healing process was slow. The fingers and the palm gradually began to come back along with the nails, but they were still unusable because he had lost all strength of his hand and could not even move it.

Amitabh had another film scheduled to start shooting: *Sharaabi*.

He was in a dilemma. What could he do? How would he shoot?

This time he came up with another style statement. He kept his damaged hand in his trouser pocket and performed all scenes, all song and dance sequences in the entire film with his left hand hidden from view.

There was one song in the movie where he had to play the *'ghungroo'* (a string of small bells), on his bare hands. He pulled out his damaged hand and hit the *ghungroos* with it. The script was for the hand to bleed because of this act and the dancer comes by and stops Amitabh's character. Amitabh's wound was still raw and so it bled and it hurt him like hell, but he still went ahead and completed the scene.

That shot in the scene was real. The blood that drips from Amitabh's hand in the film was real blood.

In Amitabh's words, "When the camera begins to roll, there is a certain madness that overcomes us. That moment in the film was one such occasion. It took me a month to get my thumb to move across and touch my index finger! And it took many months before all my fingers could get mobile and operational and many years before all the burn scars could dissolve. Till then my hand would be made up for film with make-up. But one thing did not heal – the web between the thumb and the index finger. It had melted beyond repair. So now my left hand web does not open to capacity and my index finger has become crooked."

1984: Almost exactly two years later after the Coolie accident, Amitabh was on location, shooting for film *Mard* with director Manmohan Desai in Bangalore, when there was an episode.

Returning to the hotel, while climbing the stairs to his room, without any warning, Amitabh 'just crumpled on the stairs'. He could not move. He lay there motionless unable to even raise his arms. He was then taken to his room. Two doctors were called and they examined him. There seemed to be no apparent reason for his condition. It was not a heart attack or a stroke. But Amitabh had no control over his body movements. He could not walk, could not drink water, could not brush his teeth, or even purse his lips.

It was a scary situation. It was also a freaky coincidence.

Same city, same director and filming on location.

There was panic all around. History seemed to be repeating itself.

Without wasting a single minute, Amitabh was rushed to Bombay. The superstar was back at Breach Candy Hospital, in the same room where he was just two years ago, fighting for his life. On detailed examination and tests, he was diagnosed with Myasthenia Gravis, a rare muscle dysfunctional disorder. Myas gravis what? It was a medical term very few had even heard of at that time, let alone understand what it entailed.

This was a big blow to Amitabh and his family.

This diagnosis came barely two years after he had survived an epic battle with death and nature was dealing him another blow. A rare disease that was debilitating. A condition that could prevent him from working or ever acting again. This seemed like a permanent end to his screen career.

There were about fifteen producers who had signed the superstar for forthcoming productions. They were in shock and understandably jittery. Most had borrowed at the prohibitively high-interest rates common in the industry and had paid Amitabh advance money running into several lakhs of rupees. However, only two films starring him were actually shooting; *Mard* which was 50% complete, and another film was in progress.

Speculation that Amitabh's ailment could be disastrous for the industry of which he has been the leading light for the last 10 years, were downplayed by Bombay film producers.

"The heavens are not going to fall if films are delayed for a little while, Amitabh should rest until he is completely fit. He has been overtaxing himself," said Desai.

Producer G.P. Sippy agreed: "The industry is able to adjust itself to such occurrences. I am sure he will be able to return to work in another two months."

Initial reports from the hospital were encouraging. Amitabh was responding "fairly well" to the treatment, though his asthmatic condition could cause a complication. The attending doctor remarked, "The disease is not necessarily progressively degenerative, at times there can be long remissions when it goes away completely. There is no reason why he should not return to films after a while."

According to the doctors treating Amitabh, Myasthenia is often triggered off by trauma or exhaustion. Luckily, strong drugs are usually able to keep the disability in check. Amitabh continued his treatment for a few years and went into remission.

The star himself took a gloomy view. Clearly depressed, he confided to Times of India correspondent, Khalid Mohammed: "I know I am quite ill. It doesn't look as if I will ever be able to face the camera again." He added wryly: "Anyway people are getting fed up of me doing the same role over and over again, aren't they?" His confession stunned the Bombay film industry which had until then believed that Amitabh had been admitted into the hospital for routine checks because of exhaustion.

Many years later, Amitabh wrote on his blog about his condition and his state of mind then. "If your eye shuts it cannot open on its own and if it opens it cannot close on its own; you have to use toothpicks to open them by the hand and then hold them up with the sticks." My treatment started with Mestinon, a tablet that would get me functional again and I would slip into it again as the tablet effects wore off. 8 to 10 tablets a day kept me going."

It was later discovered that Amitabh's condition was not due to Myasthenia Gravis but another ailment called 'Guillain–Barré syndrome' (GBS). GBS is a rapid-onset muscle weakness caused by the immune system damaging the peripheral nervous system. The symptoms are the same as Myasthenia Gravis.

The only respite during the time I was bedridden was an emotional Manmohan Desai who called on me and when I told him I may never walk again, said – " I will make a film with you on a wheel chair.. you will fight from a chair... and act sitting down ... **@*&*$@# .." and a few of his choicest abuses followed. He had a never say die spirit!

Myasthenia gravis is an auto-immune condition and is associated with fluctuating muscle weakness. In the initial stages of myasthenia the patient's eye movements, facial expressions, chewing, swallowing and respiration are affected, later the disease spreads to the neck, trunk, limbs and heart muscles. It is an illness characterized by muscular weakness due to a breakdown in the linkage between the nervous system and muscles.

Many after hearing these tales wonder how I am surviving. The American doctor in New York, where I had gone for an opinion on my myasthenia, wanted to see my medical report. On going through it, he had inquired – 'Is this guy still alive? I cannot suggest anything more than what he has already been treated for, but I would just like to meet the man'. I did.

The Health Woes Continued

2000: At a routine check-up, the doctors discovered that Amitabh had 'cirrhosis of the liver', where 75% of his liver was damaged. However, it was a condition that could be managed. What was however distressing was these tests also found a lump around his groin region. The doctors suspected it to be a malignant tumor and sent it for biopsy.

In Amitabh's words, "It took ten days for the results to come. Those ten days were like waiting for the guillotine. I was in the middle of KBC at the time. How would I ever be able to complete it? Chemotherapy would disfigure my face. Make up alternatives were being prepared."

While the tests were in progress, Amitabh continued filming for KBC. His dedication to his work overtakes every other emotion. Even at this stressful time, he was thinking about completing his work, about honoring his commitments. This was Amitabh's first time hosting a television show with a live audience. The episodes were filmed very close to the telecast day and Amitabh felt he could not let down the channel and the producers, due to his personal circumstances.

And so it was 'business as usual' for the show. Every evening, Amitabh was there, in front of the TV cameras with a smile on his face, a spring in his walk, and happiness in his voice. He was giving one of his best performances. Nobody knew what was going on in his mind. Nobody had any insight into the trauma Amitabh was facing. All of India were glued to their television sets - their heart-throb was in their homes every evening, entertaining them.

The stakes were high, the audience was playing the game, but it was Amitabh who had everything on the line.

The results came and they were negative for cancer. Amitabh was ecstatic and he danced with joy!

Sadly, his joys were short-lived. He started getting severe spinal pains which he attributed to spending too many hours sitting on the KBC chair, hosting the show. He started taking pain-killers to get him through the episodes. It was a grueling schedule as he was filming multiple episodes every day. It was a crazy work schedule and an unrealistic demand on the host of the show. While the crew was also part of the same schedule, they were working in shifts. The host of the show is 'the one and only'. Amitabh was in front of the cameras, giving his best performance every time, doing multiple episodes throughout the day. Not a single person ever stopped to think: Here was a 58-year-old man, on sets for more than twelve hours a day, on consecutive days. That only goes to show the calibre of the star performer!

The pain pills were taking its toll on Amitabh's liver. But he could not stop. He was in such excruciating pain that he was finding it impossible to even walk. Something had to be done. Amitabh finally decided to undergo detailed tests and was back in hospital.

The diagnosis was shattering!

Amitabh had contracted Tuberculosis (TB) of the spinal cord. But Amitabh being Amitabh, this did not stop him. He started the course of medications prescribed and, with periodic rest periods was back on his feet within a year. Amidst all of these setbacks, Amitabh has exhibited a strong exterior, a resolute attitude in his life. He has withstood a lot with his health, and has been a strong survivor through all his illnesses. He frequently writes about his health issues and how he overcame these to provide encouragement to others and spread awareness.

How many people can keep up this level of motivation? How many can maintain their enthusiasm for work in face of multiple health challenges? Amitabh's attitude is a classic example of a 'work is worship' attitude. 'Come hail or storm, one goes on. Put on the paint, get ready for the camera.'

Amitabh's son, Abhishek's response to a question on if he thought his Dad needed to slow down his work pace?

"No, not at all. Each individual knows the limits of his body and how far to push himself. My father knows his limits and has always worked within them. I feel his capacity for hard work is far beyond the normal. I hope he gets back to his normal life. Because that's what makes him happy. And I like to see him happy.

If he's happy working at the same pace as before and if that pace continues to suit him, then I'm happy. I'm sure he'll be more caring of his health now — and he always has been — not just for himself, but for all of us. The illness was not in his control. I know he takes very, very good care of himself. He is a very responsible son, husband, father and grandfather. He knows his duties towards his family and his audience.

2005: Amitabh's health failed him again. What he thought was a gastrological problem turned out to be 'Diverticulitis of the small intestine', where the walls of the large or the small intestine tend to get weaker leading to inflammation. Under normal circumstances and for many patients, antibiotics can cure it.

But Amitabh's health had taken several beatings, his immune system was compromised by the medications he was on and his body was in a fragile state. His doctors said that the ailment was rare and could have proved fatal had it not been discovered in time. Amitabh's condition was quite severe, and he had to undergo surgery. Reaching full recovery took two months in hospital.

Due to multiple surgeries to either side of his abdomen, Amitabh's stomach muscles have lost all their strength. This impacts all movements of the torso. Basic actions, like running, jumping, getting up and sitting down, all are impaired. Yet it would be impossible to tell this from watching Amitabh perform. All through these years, Amitabh continues to give superlative performances, no compromises visible, no impairment evident.

A good actor? Or a first-class fighter?

I am still searching for a parallel within performers, for someone who has enthralled his audiences around the world, conveying perfection while being an 'injured soldier' for the better part of his life on celluloid.

"I sometimes lament the fact that I do not have the benefit of a complete and ailment-free body structure, and I wonder how wonderful it would be to be normal again. But this was my fate and I shall accept it with a smile."

The Racehorse

Amitabh is a versatile actor excelling in all aspects of performing – Acting, singing, dancing, comedy, action, emotional histrionics and hosting shows. He is credited with excellent timing, an elusive quality, which is very hard to define, to nail down, to find that right moment.

Amitabh likes to eyeball the subject and the story. He is always interested and aware of nuances of his characters, so as to make them clearly distinct from one movie to the other. It was so easy for him to get stereotyped. In 1982, six of his films were released - *Satte pe Satta, Shakti, Bemisal, NamakHalal, Khuddar,* and *Desh Premi.* In three of these films, he played a double role! So he actually played nine roles in that one year!

Amitabh as an actor, goes from the great expanse of the story to the intimacy of the role. After watching him on screen, one comes away with more than just an enjoyment of the performance. One also forms emotional connections, extending from the character onto Amitabh. His heart, mind, and body are all synced as one. There is a simple honesty, bravery, and an experimental quality, all of which keeps his performances fresh – each one substantially different from the other. Amitabh loves a challenge and the artiste in him revels in travelling the character's journey.

One finds, with each passing year, with each new performance, there is something more to him. There's something yet untapped that is revealed in his next film. One gets the feeling that he thrives on that instinct to get under the skin of a new character, and to explore new shades. We, the audience, wait for each new movie with a new genre explored and something new revealed. There is always more to come.

Amitabh as an actor, as an artiste and as a person does not rest on his laurels. He is a man driven by his mind forces and is constantly inventing different traditions to explore. In Amitabh's words: "As long as there is work, I will work"!

2018 marks the beginning of Amitabh's 50th year as an artiste and he is still surprising his audiences. You only need to look at his canvas of work in the last decade or so to understand what I am alluding to: *Black, Paa, Shamitabh, Satyagraha, Piku,* Wazir, *Te3N, Sarkar3, Pink,* and the latest, *102 Not Out,* all of these, sterling performances.

My observations could be tainted by my adoration for the artiste and his craft, but I find a very deep human connection of how Amitabh the superstar and Amitabh the artiste merge with the character he portrays on screen, forming a one-to-one relationship with the viewer. Instead of the superstar taking over the character through sheer charisma, I find his personality empowers the role with a familiar affection but does not overtake it. We come away with a strong sentimental bond with the character portrayed that stays with us for a long time.

The Importance Of Family

Amitabh Bachchan has always expressed how much he values his parents' teachings and how they have been the foremost 'guru' in his life. Amitabh is inspired by his father's poems and literary works and they have served him well in every walk of his life. Time and time again, his actions have shown how he has taken courage and motivation from his father's teachings. They have stood by him through the peaks and troughs of what life has challenged him with, facing life's fortunes and calamities with fortitude.

For many, even today, Amitabh's greatest recommendation is to be the son of Harivansh Rai Bachchan. In an earlier blog post, Amitabh recalls, "Both my parents are extremely strong people. My father, of course, is less vocal, but his sheer presence exudes discipline. Everybody shuddered at his discipline. Later on, of course, he sobered down. But even now he has an open mind. Whenever he decides on something, his word is final, nobody can change it. But my mother tells me he had a very strong temper. My brother and I used to shudder at the thought of even having to present ourselves in front of him."

As with all good things, the blessings and guidance of parents are missed most when they are not there. There are times when life throws you into a quandary, and you think, "I wish they were here to give me advice" or "What would they have done in this situation?" Amitabh had imbibed many lessons and much culture from his parents early on in life. It's clear that his thoughts are deeply influenced by their philosophies and his actions steeped in their ideologies.

In recent times, with the rise of the nuclear family model, urban India is facing an erosion of family values due to a dominance of the materialistic and self-absorbed approach of society. Amitabh is a firm believer in the joint family, or the extended family system. In his view, parents selflessly spend their entire life and all their savings to raise their children in their best capacity and it is the duty of the following generation to look after their aging parents and elders, when the need arises. Indian culture, as a tradition, supports the joint family system and teaches us to look after our parents when they need us most.

It is a known fact that during Amitabh's father's illness, he spent sleepless nights being at his father's bedside. Amitabh had created a virtual intensive care unit at home, with all the top medical facilities and took special care of his father's needs.

Fame, reputation and material wealth; these are transitory. What really matters and stays with you for life are values, culture, family, togetherness, and strength of character.

In response to the question, 'Does Abhishek remind you of the younger Amitabh Bachchan?' the proud father shines through, "Abhishek is a far better version than what I was at his age. I don't possess his physique, or those intense, powerful eyes he's inherited from his mother. He moves and dances better than me and I am envious of that. In all respects he is much more complete than I was. Every time we sit at home and discuss him, Jaya always taunts me by saying, 'What were you doing in your 11th film? Just look at that again and stop criticizing the little fellow.' That is a fact. I am still awkward in many situations, but Abhishek handles it all comfortably."

A Survivor To This Day

"Out of suffering have emerged the strongest souls; the most massive characters are seared with scars."

Kahlil Gibran

The mid to late 90s were some of the darkest hours for Amitabh. He might have recovered from his medical ordeal, but the struggles weren't over. His films were flopping and his company was falling apart. Those who wanted him to fail were having a field day while his debts continued to grow.

In 1999, ABCL sought protection under the bankruptcy laws. The Bombay High Court restrained Amitabh from selling off his assets until loan recovery cases and debts were dealt with. Of this time, Amitabh said: "Our friends advised us to close this losing venture and move on but we decided to clear all our debts despite huge losses and re-start the production of films."

"It is only my conscience that kept me going," the legendary actor explained. "Many businessmen and financial advisers told me that I should give up ABCL and start a new life. But somewhere I felt that I owe people money. People had put faith in ABCL because of my name. Therefore, I could not let it go easily."

"There was a sword hanging on my head all the time. I spent many sleepless nights."

At this time, Amitabh was the only earning member of his family, his wife having retired from the film industry and his son yet to gain a footing. It's hard to imagine how he would have felt with this financial burden hanging over his head. Although he had played varied difficult roles with aplomb in his acting career, his 'role' in real life had experienced many setbacks. His entrepreneurship didn't go the way he had planned. He had even attempted a forgettable stint in politics in the late 80s.

At this dark hour in his life, he refused to give up, and came to a momentous decision. It was time, he thought, to return to what he did best.

Amitabh approached Yash Chopraji, one of the most respected film-makers in the industry, and with whom he had done three award-winning movies. He set aside his pride and frankly laid bare his current situation, how he was bankrupt and had no upcoming films. Yashji heard him out and almost immediately offered Amitabh a role to play the part of an obstinate patriarch in his film 'Mohabattein' (Love), that was due to be released in the year 2000. This movie became the turning point in Amitabh's film career and he hasn't looked back since. He said, "I then started doing commercials, television, and films. And I am happy to say today that I have repaid my entire debt of Rs. 90 crore (900 million) and am starting afresh."

It was awkward. I came to Bombay with a driving license, and that's about it. I said if I don't become an actor, I will drive a cab. I had a desire to work in the movies. I didn't have a place to stay and I spent many nights on the benches of Marine Drive with some of the largest rats I have seen in my life. The whole intention was to act. They were rough times, but I had landed up, as I said, with my driver's license and said that if I didn't make it as an actor, I would ply taxis.

Amitabh, like many, encountered struggles throughout his life. It would be easy to give up in the face of hardships, but to fight it and overcome these struggles is the ultimate act of courage. It's about determination, persistence, resilience and the will to do what it takes to get back on track. Amitabh's optimistic spirit in the face of trials both large and small is the magnet that draws so many to him. Where others would simply accept defeat, wallow in pity and lament their misfortunes, Amitabh learned from his downturns, faced his struggles head-on and rose from darkness, stronger than before.

Amitabh Bachchan is an incredibly accomplished actor and a human being totally committed to his family and profession. Laser focused, intelligent, creative, very funny, mischief-making and at times downright crazy, Amitabh has lived his life with gusto, facing its hard knocks and highs head-on. There seems to be no obstacle too great if Amitabh sets his mind to something and that is the hallmark of a SURVIVOR.

Troubles and misfortunes are all a part of life. There are no paths which are void of obstacles. It's a duty we bear on ourselves, man or woman, to keep focused on the chosen path, overcoming each hurdle. Daylight always follows darkness and without sadness, one would be unable to appreciate happiness. The euphoria of success would be a flat feeling in the absence of the pain or despondency of failure.

Life may take downturns, but to show strength of character in the face of defeat is an envious quality and one that all of mankind would be gifted to possess. However, it is not often that one sees that, and this is what makes Amitabh a remarkable man – "a true survivor."

Here is an excerpt from Dr. Harivansh Rai Bachchan's poem, Amitabh's father and the famous and revered literary poet. This sums up the defining trait of a survivor well and provides direction, serving as guidance for life that we all can follow.

HIMMAT KARNE WALON KI HAAR NAHI HOTI

(Whoever acts with courage, does not lose)

Jab tak na safal ho, neend chain ko tyaago tum,

Sangharsh ka maidaan chhodh kar mat bhaago tum.

Kuch kiye bina hi jai jai kaar nahi hoti,

Koshish karne walon ki kabhi haar nahi hoti.

Translated

Till you don't succeed, sacrifice your sleep and peace,

From the battlefield of struggle, don't run away.

Without making required efforts, there are no accolades to be won,

People who try and persevere, will never fail.

Courtesy: Excerpt from Dr. Harivansh Rai Bachchan's poem:
'Himmat Karne Walon Ki Haar Nahi Hoti'

EPIGRAPH

AUGUST 2ND, EVERY YEAR

Amitabh has not forgotten the day of his "rebirth". "If I am here before you answering your questions, it is undoubtedly because of the incredible efficiency of the doctors at the hospital, and the millions of prayers that went up from my well-wishers all over the world. That is a debt I shall never be able to repay."

http://srbachchan.tumblr.com

Every year, Amitabh remembers the day of his "rebirth"

From his Facebook page post:
"Aug 2, the day I lived again ... my Coolie accident ... brought to Breach Candy Hospital, Mumbai and second surgery performed, where when I did not come out, was clinically dead for a few minutes ... so many that know wish me a Happy Birthday for today. Many thanks in advance, for it was the prayers of millions of my countrymen that saved my life."

Sunday evenings are the adrenalin, not just for me but for any public figure, when the people support and affection comes voluntarily. Enthusiastic, warm loving and boisterous!!

Security and staff get that weekly opportunity to flex their muscles in keeping the crowds at bay and I get the opportunity to flex my fingers in autograph signing!!

A warm lovely moment and I am always surprised how this has lasted for so long. From 1982 to date. That's 36 years!! Goodness that's a lifetime! God has been kind and very gracious.

Many among you now after reading this report would be sick and disgusted by it – it does not make good copy. But if anyone were to ask me now how I was still alive, I would not hesitate to tell them it's because of my extended family my EF, my FmXt !!

EPILOGUE

One evening, at home in Bombay (Mumbai) but I am old school and it's still Bombay for me, a dear friend calls me out of the blue and says, 'Hey Raju (my nickname), would you like to meet Mr. Amitabh Bachchan?" There were five seconds of silence followed by hysterical screams, yes, yes, of course yes, hell yes!!

My friend laughed saying, "Oh, I thought you had grown out of your teenage crush but looks like you are still enamored by him. Ok, dear girl, today is your lucky day as you have got your wish. You can accompany me to the sets tomorrow and after the shoot, you may be able to meet him". So the very next day, I reach Film City where 'Kaun Banega Crorepati' the Indian version of 'Who wants to be a Millionaire' is being filmed and Mr. Bachchan is the ever charming, ever handsome host.

On this day, 6th September 2011, Mr. Bachchan was shooting three episodes and was on the set from 6 am, expecting to finish around 8 pm. I reached the soundstage around 5 pm, not wanting to be late.

Sitting there, separate from the audience in a special enclosure meant for guests, I waited for that moment when I would lay my eyes on him for the first time. My heart was beating very fast and adrenaline coursed through my body. There was a steady murmur on the sets, crew moving around setting up their positions, and endless instructions fired through headsets. Then suddenly, there was a big hush and almost immediately, an eerie silence. Just then, as if on cue, Amitabh walked in, through the corridors straight to the main arena.

His pace was very fast and his gait long as he walked to his center seat and addressed the audience, but for me, it seemed like he was speaking directly to me through the sharp microphones of the set, his rich baritone a personal voice in my ear.

Here was my idol, in flesh and blood, almost 35 years since I first saw him on screen. This time it was not the big screen, the TV or my cell phone. This person was on stage there, about ten feet away from me. And he was so alive. So dynamic. There was an energy to him that permeated through that space and touched me.

The shoot went on for almost six hours, ending at midnight and I just sat there taking in every word, every nuance, every inflection in his voice. This was real. This was like watching a performance seated in the front row. I was over the moon.

Then, as the audience walked out, the few of us seated in the enclosure were asked to go over to him for an opportunity to say hello, one at a time.

I was the last one in line and I waited, silently. The only sound I could hear was my heart beating loud and fast. I was sure everyone else could hear it too. I had no idea what I would say.

Would he shake hands with me?

Would I say hello, very nice to meet you?

Or would he just nod, acknowledge me and that would be it?

My hands were cold and trembling but my face was flushed and hot. Then suddenly, I was looking straight at his necktie as he towered tall above me.

He looked at me, shook my hand and said, "Hello, you all have been waiting so long. Let's just take a seat here." And before I knew it, I was sitting right next to him!

That's when I found my voice. I said, "Actually, I've been waiting almost 30 years to see you and talk to you". He looked at me incredulously and said, "Oh my Gosh! That's a lifetime. It's too much pressure on me now."

I replied, "I am so happy, so thrilled to be able to meet with you, to talk with you. A dream of mine has come true today". He said, "I am glad I did not disappoint". He spoke to me for a few seconds, asking what I do and where I live. Then with a firm handshake, a very warm smile, and his penetrating eyes, he said: "Goodbye, all the very best".

I was a very happy girl, not just on that night but for a long, long time.

But this wasn't the only time Amitabh Bachchan's world and my world met. My family's connection with Amitabh Bachchan actually goes back to the days when he was just getting started in the film industry. We lived in Colaba, South Bombay in 'Usha Sadan' building, and for some time, Amitabh stayed at the opposite 'Sunita Apartments'.

'Usha Sadan' was then home to a few film personalities, like Jeetendra, the actor; Kailash Chopra, the producer; Sheila Jones, the model; and Jitendra Arya, the iconic photographer; to name a few.

Those were the swinging seventies, and fashion and films ruled. It was here that my Mum and Aunty occasionally spotted a very young Amitabh, either meeting Jeetendra or Sheila Jones, his friend from his Calcutta days.

There would be a constant stream of film personalities to Usha Sadan and within this crowd, Amitabh stood out – with his tall, lithe frame, on a motorcycle, appearing very refined and urbane, easily charming the gawking teenage girls of the building complex (my two aunties included).

Kailash and Prem Chopra's wives and Jeetendra's sister were good friends with our family and they would come home often for kitty parties (a very social event). As kids at home, we would sneak up to where the guests were (we had a curfew time of 7 pm to be home) and would hear conversations which mostly revolved around film happenings, latest gossip, who was going around with whom, invites to opening nights and movie launches. This was in the mid-seventies, so there was no internet and no television and it was all about hearsay. Amitabh and Jeetendra were the favorite celebrities as they had a few of their films released around then and so these two actors were the most talked about at these social gatherings.

That, dear readers, was my first introduction to the world of films and celebrities. It was later grown into a lifelong passion after my Dad became a producer and started making films. Though my career resides within the sphere of business, cyber and technology, I have never really left the world of films. I kept up my connection by learning about filmmaking, doing film reviews and now, writing this book.

THE CHARITY

I lost both my parents to illness, way too early in life and for reasons that were easily preventable. My mother's sudden passing away (1993) and my Dad's gradual health decline and subsequent passing away (2008), both could have been prevented if we had timely access to the correct diagnosis, required funds, and necessary treatment.

On both occasions, we could generate the needed resources and medical advice, but it was not enough. Despite not having the right access, we were still considered lucky and fortunate because we, the three siblings, were educated, smart, and considerably well informed. But still, it was not good enough. It was not at all enough to navigate the convoluted medical administration, the nexus between hospitals and doctors, the expensive tests, and the plethora of medications prescribed. We could see that all of it was done without a holistic concern and little regard to the overall impact on the person being treated. My experience and the saga of what we as a family went through those times can easily fill another book.

EPILOGUE

During an interview in 1983, Amitabh admitted that he realized how he was privileged to have the best of medicines, being imported from abroad, while others who did not have the luxury, suffered haplessly. Amitabh talked at length about the transformation he underwent post the Coolie accident:-

"There were people who want to know details as to how it all happened and whether it was the punch or the table or whatever, and I tell them that it's not important as to how I was injured, but what really is important is the lack of medical facility after I was injured and what made me really aware of these factors when I was in the hospital was that we sadly lack timely facility towards people who might be in similar condition that I was.

I find that we have the brain and the talent amongst us to cope with any emergency. But we lack in facility, we lack in equipment and perhaps finance to set up this equipment. When I was in hospital there was help coming from every quarter, and I want to say in all immodesty that there was help coming from abroad, there were doctors flown in from London. There was medicine coming in from Singapore, England and America because I have the financial capacity… but what if it wasn't me, what if it was an ordinary poor man on the streets, who's in similar condition.

Would he be able to afford similar treatment? Had he not been able to afford, what would have been his end. And that was one of the things that was most distressing."

Amitabh shares an anecdote - *"There was a girl, I remember in Breach Candy with me. She is about 3 years old. She had been admitted for gangrene in her lower portion. And one of the doctors was telling me that there are medicines coming in for you every day, do you think it's possible for you to get a particular medicine for this patient, this girl, who's almost certainly going to die because she has reached a stage where we can't cure it now? And I said yes medicines were coming every day. We got the medicine for her the next day. She was cured and she went home in three days. And I was very happy for her. What distressed me was the reaction of her mother when the doctor went and told her that we have tried a new medicine that has been flown in for you. The mother said whoever is getting this medicine, and wherever it's coming from, don't tell me its cost because I won't be able to afford it. And*

157

tell the person who got the medicine to pay up. This really distressed me because I wonder how many people in our country are going through this."

And this is when I knew what would be the most appropriate use for the profits generated from this book. It will be used to supplement local charities who help those that have relatives in hospital and assist them with support facilities and coordination with medical staff so they can get the right help at the right time.

ACKNOWLEDGEMENTS

This book has been made possible with the support and efforts of people coming together as a team for this unique endeavor and I would like to individually thank:

Mr. Amitabh Bachchan, for his blessings and very kind gesture in penning his thoughts for the foreword.

Rosy Singh, Mr. Bachchan's Chief Executive Secretary, for her time in helping with permissions and providing timely assistance with my requests.

Andy McDermott, of Publicious, for his expert advice and guidance in my first ever publishing effort.

Amy Sincock, for her second pair of eyes, periodically "pulling me out of the past and into the present", and keeping me honest with her objectivity.

Vicky Lalsinghani, for his microscopic scrutiny of the book, highlighting omissions and details missed by human eyes and software combined.

Anita Patel, for her behind the scenes help in magically making things happen and keeping me on track.

Subhash, Adesh and Rakesh, from the AB Corp. office, for being so courteous and helpful.

Lisa McAskill, for her mentoring, support and expert guidance in the making of the book promotion video and film review clips.

Harvey Newland-Harman, a teenage genius, for his clever work with the camera and intuitive editing with all my review videos.

And most important of all:

My family, especially my brother Vicky Lalsinghani, my sister Mona Punjabi and my nephew Khush Punjabi for putting up with my erratic, sometimes rude, sometimes freaked out behavior, whilst rushing against time to complete this book.

Finally, a big thank you to the free press of India and to world journalism for carrying the mantle of reporting; of being the trusted source of information in the world of fake news and for spearheading mass movements. Newspapers have an immense responsibility as they are still the most important medium at the forefront, accessing information, analyzing it, uncovering the truth, and making it public knowledge.

REMARKABLE FILM CAREER

Completing 49 years of being in films with over 200 appearances! On to Karan Johar's trilogy 'Brahmastra' releasing in 2019.

FB 1915 - 49 years ago I came to the city of dreams, Mumbai and signed my 1st film 'Saat Hindustani' FEB 15, 1969, whew!!! that is a long time

Picture courtesy: Amitabh Bachchan Facebook Photo album
https://www.facebook.com/AmitabhBachchan/posts/1929922540374859

Year	As Actor in Film	Additional roles/ Special mention / Notes
2018	Badla	Shoot in progress – scheduled for 2019 release
2018	Thugs of Hindostan	Shoot in progress - December 2018 release
2018	102 Not Out	Released on 4th May 2018
2018	Pad Man	Special appearance
2017	Firangi	Narrator
2017	Sarkar 3	
2017	Begum Jaan	Narrator
2017	The Ghazi Attack	Narrator - Telugu and Hindi Bilingual film
2016	Pink	Nominated—Filmfare Award for Best Actor
2016	Te3n	
2016	Ki & Ka	Special appearance
2016	Wazir	
2015	Piku	National Film Award for Best Actor Filmfare Critics Award for Best Actor Nominated—Filmfare Award for Best Actor
2015	Hey Bro	Special appearance in song "Birju"
2015	Shamitabh	And playback singer for song "Piddly" And Producer
2014	Manam	Special appearance -Telugu film
2014	Bhoothnath Returns	
2013	Mahabharat	Animated film
2013	Krrish 3	Narrator
2013	Boss	Narrator
2013	Satyagraha	
2013	Bombay Talkies	Special appearance on segment "Murabba"
2013	The Great Gatsby	Special appearance - Hollywood Film
2012	English Vinglish	Special appearance
2012	Bol Bachchan	Playback singer and appeared in song "Bol Bachchan"
2012	Department	
2012	Mr. Bhatti on Chutti	Special appearance
2012	Kahaani	Playback singer for song "Ekla Chalo Re"
2011	Ra.One	Narrator
2011	Aarakshan	Nominated—Filmfare Award for Best Actor
2011	Buddah Hoga Terra Baap	And playback singer for song "Bbuddah Hoga Terra Baap" And Producer
2010	Kandahar	Malayalam film
2010	Teen Patti	
2010	Rann	

2009	Paa	National Film Award for Best Actor Filmfare Award for Best Actor And playback singer for "Mere Paa" And Producer
2009	Aladin	And playback singer for "Genie Rap" & "O re Sawariya"
2009	Zor Lagaa Ke...Haiya!	Narrator
2009	Delhi-6	Special appearance And playback singer for "Noor"
2008	God Tussi Great Ho	
2008	Sarkar Raj	
2008	Bhoothnath	And playback singer for "Mere Buddy" & "Chalo Jaane Do"
2008	Yaar Meri Zindagi	
2008	Jodhaa Akbar	Narrator
2007	Om Shanti Om	Special appearance
2007	The Last Lear	English language film
2007	Aag	
2007	Jhoom Barabar Jhoom	Cameo appearance and singer for 'Jhoom'
2007	Swami	Narrator
2007	Shootout at Lokhandwala	
2007	Cheeni Kum	
2007	Ek Krantiveer	Narrator - Marathi film
2007	Nishabd	
2007	Eklavya: The Royal Guard	
2006	Baabul	And playback singer for "Come On"
2006	Ganga	Bhojpuri film
2006	Kabhi Alvida Naa Kehna	Nominated—Filmfare Award for Best Supporting Actor
2006	Amrutha Varsham	Special appearance - Telugu film
2006	Darna Zaroori Hai	Appeared in one segment
2006	Family	And Producer
2005	Ek Ajnabee	
2005	Amrithadhare	Special appearance - Kannada film
2005	Dil Jo Bhi Kahey	
2005	Ramji Londonwale	Special appearance
2005	Viruddh- Family Comes First	And Producer
2005	Sarkar	Nominated—Filmfare Award for Best Actor
2005	Paheli	
2005	Parineeta	Narrator
2005	Bunty Aur Babli	Nominated—Filmfare Award for Best Supporting Actor
2005	Waqt: The Race Against Time	

Year	Film	Notes
2005	Black	National Film Award for Best Actor Filmfare Award for Best Actor Filmfare Critics Award for Best Actor
2004	Ab Tumhare Hawale Watan Saathiyo	
2004	Veer-Zaara	Nominated—Filmfare Award for Best Supporting Actor
2004	Hum Kaun Hai?	
2004	Kyun! Ho Gaya Na...	
2004	Deewaar	
2004	Lakshya	
2004	Dev	
2004	Insaaf: The Justice	Narrator
2004	Rudraksh	Narrator
2004	Aetbaar	And singer for "Jeena Hai"
2004	Khakee	Nominated—Filmfare Award for Best Actor
2003	Fun 2shh: Dudes in the 10th Century	Narrator
2003	Baghban	Nominated—Filmfare Award for Best Actor and playback singer for: "Chali Chali" , "Holi Khele", "Main Yaha"
2003	Boom	
2003	Mumbai Se Aaya Mera Dost	Narrator
2003	Armaan	And singer for "Aao Milke Gaye"
2003	Khushi	Narrator
2002	Kaante	Nominated—Filmfare Award for Best Actor
2002	Agni Varsha	
2002	Hum Kisise Kum Nahin	
2002	Aankhen	Nominated—Filmfare Award for Best Supporting Actor
2001	Kabhi Khushi Kabhie Gham	Nominated—Filmfare Award for Best Supporting Actor And singer for "Shava Shava"
2001	Aks	Filmfare Critics Award for Best Actor Nominated—Filmfare Award for Best Actor and And Producer
2001	Lagaan	Narrator
2001	Ek Rishtaa: The Bond of Love	
2000	Mohabbatein	Filmfare Award for Best Supporting Actor
1999	Hello Brother	Narrator
1999	Kohram	

1999	Hindustan Ki Kasam	
1999	Biwi No.1	Special appearance
1999	Sooryavansham	And singer for "Chori Se"
1999	Lal Baadshah	
1998	Hero Hindustani	Narrator
1998	Bade Miyan Chote Miyan	
1998	Major Saab	And Producer
1997	Mrityudata	And Producer
1996	Tere Mere Sapne	Narrator and Producer
1996	Ghatak: Lethal	Special appearance
1994	Akka	Special appearance - Marathi film
1994	Insaniyat	
1993	Professor Ki Padosan	Special appearance
1992	Zulm Ki Hukumat	Narrator
1992	Khuda Gawah	Nominated—Filmfare Award for Best Actor
1991	Akayla	
1991	Indrajeet	
1991	Ajooba	
1991	Hum	Filmfare Award for Best Actor
1990	Aaj Ka Arjun	
1990	Kroadh	Special appearance
1990	Agneepath	National Film Award for Best Actor Nominated—Filmfare Award for Best Actor
1989	Main Azaad Hoon	And playback singer for "Itne Baazu"
1989	Jaadugar	And playback singer for "Padosan Apni Murgi"
1989	Batwara	Narrator
1989	Toofan	
1988	Soorma Bhopali	Special appearance
1988	Gangaa Jamunaa Saraswati	
1988	Hero Hiralal	Special appearance
1988	Shahenshah	Nominated—Filmfare Award for Best Actor
1988	Kaun Jeeta Kaun Haara	Special appearance And playback singer for "Jeevan pyar bina"
1987	Jalwa	Special appearance
1986	Aakhree Raasta	
1985	Mard	Nominated—Filmfare Award for Best Actor
1985	Ghulami	Narrator
1985	Geraftaar	

165

1984	Sharaabi	Nominated—Filmfare Award for Best Actor
1984	Pet Pyaar Aur Paap	Guest appearance
1984	Paan Khaye Saiyan Hamaar	Special appearance
1984	Kanoon Kya Karega	Narrator
1984	Khabardar	Incomplete
1984	Inquilaab	
1983	Coolie	
1983	Pukar	And playback singer for "Tu maike mat jaiyo"
1983	Mahaan	
1983	Andha Kanoon	Guest appearance
1983	Nastik	
1982	Shakti	Nominated—Filmfare Award for Best Actor
1982	Khud-Daar	
1982	Namak Halaal	Nominated—Filmfare Award for Best Actor
1982	Desh Premee	
1982	Bemisal	Nominated—Filmfare Award for Best Actor
1982	Satte Pe Satta	
1981	Vilayati Babu	Special appearance - Punjabi film
1981	Kaalia	
1981	Silsila	Nominated—Filmfare Award for Best Actor And playback singer for: "Neela Aasman" "Rang Barse Bhige Chunar Wali"
1981	Lawaaris	Nominated—Filmfare Award for Best Actor And playback singer for song "Mere Angene Mein"
1981	Chashme Buddoor	Special appearance
1981	Naseeb	And playback singer for "Chal mere bhai"
1981	Barsaat Ki Ek Raat	
1981	Yaarana	
1981	Commander	Special appearance
1980	Shaan	
1980	Ram Balram	
1980	Dostana	Nominated—Filmfare Award for Best Actor
1980	Do Aur Do Paanch	
1979	Suhaag	
1979	Kaala Patthar	Nominated—Filmfare Award for Best Actor

1979	Mr. Natwarlal	Nominated—Filmfare Award for Best Male Playback Singer Nominated—Filmfare Award for Best Actor And singer for "Mere Pas Aao"
1979	Manzil	
1979	Jurmana	
1979	Ahsaas	Special appearance
1979	Gol Maal	Special appearance
1979	The Great Gambler	And singer for "Do Lafzon Ki"
1978	Muqaddar Ka Sikandar	Nominated—Filmfare Award for Best Actor
1978	Don	Filmfare Award for Best Actor
1978	Trishul	Nominated—Filmfare Award for Best Actor
1978	Besharam	
1978	Kasme Vaade	
1978	Ganga Ki Saugandh	
1977	Alaap	
1977	Chala Murari Hero Banne	Special appearance
1977	Parvarish	
1977	Shatranj Ke Khilari	Narrator
1977	Khoon Pasina	
1977	Immaan Dharam	
1977	Amar Akbar Anthony	Filmfare Award for Best Actor
1977	Charandas	Special appearance in song "'Dekh Lo"
1976	Balika Badhu	
1976	Adalat	Nominated—Filmfare Award for Best Actor
1976	Hera Pheri	
1976	Kabhie Kabhie	Nominated—Filmfare Award for Best Actor
1976	Do Anjaane	
1975	Mili	
1975	Chupke Chupke	
1975	Chhoti Si Baat	Special Appearance
1975	Faraar	
1975	Sholay	
1975	Zameer	
1975	Deewaar	Nominated—Filmfare Award for Best Actor
1974	Majboor	
1974	Kunwara Baap	Special appearance
1974	Roti Kapda Aur Makaan	
1974	Benaam	

1974	Kasauti	
1974	Dost	Special appearance
1973	Bada Kabutar	Special appearance
1973	Namak Haraam	Filmfare Award for Best Actor
1973	Saudagar	
1973	Abhimaan	
1973	Gehri Chaal	
1973	Bandhe Haath	
1973	Zanjeer	Nominated—Filmfare Award for Best Actor
1972	Jaban	Special appearance
1972	Garam Masala	Special appearance
1972	Raaste Kaa Patthar	
1972	Ek Nazar	
1972	Bansi Birju	
1972	Bawarchi	Narrator
1972	Bombay to Goa	
1972	Piya Ka Ghar	Special appearance
1972	Sanjog	
1971	Guddi	Special appearance
1971	Reshma Aur Shera	
1971	Pyar Ki Kahani	
1971	Anand	Filmfare Award for Best Actor
1971	Parwana	
1970	Bombay Talkie	Special appearance
1969	Bhuvan Shome	Narrator
1969	Saat Hindustani	National Film Award for Best Newcomer

REFERENCES

1. https://www.facebook.com/AmitabhBachchan/

2. https://en.wikipedia.org/wiki/Amitabh_Bachchan

3. https://en.wikipedia.org/wiki/Harivansh_Rai_Bachchan

4. https://www.indiatvnews.com/entertainment/celebrities-amitabh-bachchan-birthday-special-when-big-b-injured-on-coolie-sets-in-1982-405955

5. http://movies.ndtv.com/bollywood/the-day-amitabh-bachchan-lived-again-august-2-613181

6. https://www.hindustantimes.com/entertainment/amitabh-bachchan-got-liver-cirrhosis-from-coolie-accident/story-iYhe2JrnPzscbO6esAjl4K.html

7. https://www.bemoneyaware.com/blog/amitabh-bachchan-from-bankruptcy-to-crorepati/

8. https://www.filmibeat.com/television/news/2010/kbc-savior-amitabh-300910.html

9. https://www.thequint.com/news/india/how-amitabhs-mom-teji-helped-sonia-rajiv-get-married

10. https://timesofindia.indiatimes.com/entertainment/hindi/bollywood/news/Amitabh-first-met-Rajiv-when-he-was-4-years-old/articleshow/9344149.cms

11. http://www.sify.com/movies/teji-bachchan-indira-s-friend-news-bollywood-kkfulwhfgfhsi.html

12. https://economictimes.indiatimes.com/articleshow/219328.cms?utm_source=contentofinterest&utm_medium=text&utm_campaign=cppst

13. https://www.scoopwhoop.com/10-Harivansh-Rai-Bachchans-Best-Poems/#.n41no0kj1

14. https://economictimes.indiatimes.com/its-all-in-the-name-abcl-now-goes-as-ab-corp/articleshow/222739.cms

15. http://www.forbesindia.com/lists/1

16. http://news.bbc.co.uk/2/hi/south_asia/394226.stm

17. http://news.bbc.co.uk/2/hi/entertainment/2319917.stm

18. http://www.indiantelevision.com/headlines/y2k2/oct/oct35.htm

19. https://en.wikipedia.org/wiki/Kaun_Banega_Crorepati

20. https://www.firstpost.com/entertainment/how-kaun-banega-crorepati-revived-amitabh-bachchans-career-and-sony-tvs-ratings-4148813.html
21. https://en.wikipedia.org/wiki/Coolie_(1983_Hindi_film)
22. https://www.hindustantimes.com/india/family-values-first-big-b/story-cTEC310FF5GQiumL8NU1gM.html
23. https://www.ibtimes.co.in/i-was-clinically-dead-for-a-couple-of-minutes-says-amitabh-bachchan-392876
24. https://www.hindustantimes.com/india/big-b-s-real-life-fight/story-CAFS0mC5qG5rIA64rS1vfP.html
25. https://www.indiatoday.in/magazine/indiascope/story/19840630-amitabh-bachchan-hospitalised-for-treatment-of-rare-muscle-disease-myasthenia-gravis-803061-1984-06-30
26. http://www.bollywoodlife.com/news-gossip/sultan-salman-khan-dedicates-a-message-for-shahenshah-amitabh-bachchan-on-his-75th-birthday/
27. https://www.thequint.com/entertainment/amitabh-bachchan-remembers-the-original-showman-manmohan-desai
28. https://www.rediff.com/movies/2002/oct/10shah.htm
29. https://www.vogue.in/content/shweta-bachchan-nandas-ode-to-amitabh-bachchan/#s-cust0
30. http://www.rediff.com/movies/2005/dec/19abhishek.htm
31. https://en.wikipedia.org/wiki/Amitabh_Bachchan_filmography
32. Times of India newspaper print editions
33. Indian Express newspaper print editions
34. Mid-Day newspaper print editions

About The Author

Rajnni's passion for Bollywood comes from a strong familial tie with the film industry. Her father was a Bollywood film producer, and she spent many days of her early childhood on film sets, paying close attention to everything that was going on around her.

Although she "grew up" to be an Information Systems Auditor and Technology Project Manager by profession, Rajnni's love for everything 'Amitabh Bachchan' is what has brought this book to you.

After completing her MBA degree, Rajnni was working within the corporate sector and the world of computers but she soon realized she was hiding behind blinking screens and cyber hacks. However, her heart always yearned to go back to her passion for films. As a way to immerse herself back in the world that she loved, she started writing film reviews which found a ready audience. Thrilled with this reception, she decided to pursue her passion further, took a sabbatical from work and landed at New York University to study film-making.

Finally, in writing, she has found an outward expression for her creativity and passion. This love for film combined with an understanding of the complexities of how this industry comes together makes Rajnni a true film aficionado.

*Let yourself be silently drawn by the strange pull of what you love. It will not let you astray. When you let go of who you are, you become who you might be.....***RUMI**

www.rajnni.com

171

www.ingramcontent.com/pod-product-compliance
Lightning Source LLC
Chambersburg PA
CBHW061230150426
42812CB00054BA/2549

* 9 7 8 0 6 4 8 3 6 6 2 0 1 *